DEVELOPING
WRESTLING
CHAMPIONS

DEVELOPING
WRESTLING
CHAMPIONS

The Total Program Approach

Dariel W. Daniel

authorHOUSE®

AuthorHouse™
1663 Liberty Drive
Bloomington, IN 47403
www.authorhouse.com
Phone: 1-800-839-8640

Published by AuthorHouse 05/14/2013

ISBN: 978-1-4772-2121-1 (sc)
ISBN: 978-1-4772-2122-8 (e)

Library of Congress Control Number: 2012911482

ACKNOWLEDGEMENTS

A Special Word of Appreciation to many of those who made this publication possible:

My Family—For their many sacrifices during my coaching career.

Coach Gary Johnson—For starting the wrestling program at Troup High School in 1963.

Coach Arnold 'Swede' Umbach—For all his efforts to develop me as a wrestler and to mentor me as a coach.

Craig Garner, Beasey Hendrix - My loyal and dedicated assistants who always supported me and worked hard to help develop WRESTLING CHAMPIONS.

The thousands of wrestlers, parents, and fans who support me and my teams throughout the years.

Thanks to the following wrestlers in the technique photos:

Jarrod Trotter—2X Texas State Champion

Ophir Bernstein—Texas State Champion

Sky Walker—Texas State Champion

Joey McFarland—Allen HS, TX Wrestler

Photographer: Dusty Parrish, Allen HS, TX

Cover Photographer: Don Neuberg, LaGrange, GA

A WORD FROM THE AUTHOR

After being introduced to 'real' wrestling as a sophomore in high school by Coach Gary Johnson, I fell in love with the sport. I had 'rassled' on the red Georgia clay with my two brothers throughout my childhood and love the competition. Weighing a solid 125 pounds, and blessed with 'country strength', I decided, "This is the sport for me".

After a successful high school career, I attended Auburn University and wrestled for four years under the Southern legend, Arnold W. 'Swede' Umbach. After graduation, I worked two years with Coach Umbach as a graduate assistant, learning from one of the real masters of the sport.

The knowledge passed on to me from Coach Johnson and Coach Umbach has been invaluable in my accomplishments as a wrestler, a teacher, and a coach.

It is my intention, by writing this book, to pass on the knowledge I acquired from my coaches, rivals, peers, tapes, books, DVD's, and clinics to the next generation of wrestling coaches.

This publication is a comprehensive guide for developing wrestling champions through a proven system of technique, drills, mental skill exercises, practice organization, motivation methods, fund raising ideas, promotional ideas, conditioning games and more. You will learn the little 'secrets' that I have learned during my coaching career which has spanned four decades.

Hopefully, some part of the information presented will help you in your efforts in 'Developing Wrestling Champions' through the 'Total Program Approach'

Dariel Daniel

If you have knowledge, let others light their candle at it.

-Thomas Fuller

DEDICATION

Since my coaching career began, I have had the opportunity to work with many athletes of varying abilities and levels of dedication. The greatest honor I had was that of being able to coach my own son. It was the toughest part of my career, yet the most rewarding.

My son was Varsity for three years and never missed a single day of high school practice, although we were able to practice seven days a week. He was diligent in Freestyle/ Greco practice and attended every tournament the club could make on a local, state and national level.

He was dedicated to off-season weight training and even ran cross country for weight control and endurance training.

For these reasons, it is with great love and tremendous pride that I dedicate this publication to 3X All-State wrestler, but more importantly, my son:

Patrick Dustin 'Dusty' Daniel

ABOUT THE AUTHOR

Dariel Daniel was twice named National High School 'Coach of the Year' by WrestlingUSA magazine and the National High School Athletic Coaches Association. As head coach, his teams won nine State Championships in Georgia and five in Texas where he served as an assistant.

Daniel recently retired from teaching after forty years and currently resides in LaGrange, GA. He stays involved in wrestling by officiating and presenting free camps and clinics for local athletes.

ABOUT THE BOOK

Developing Wrestling Champions
The Total Program Approach

With a coaching career that spanned four decades, Daniel has developed a comprehensive guide guaranteed to producing championship caliber wrestlers year after year. Several publications have discussed specific areas of a total program including technique, fund raising, drills, games, nutrition and mental skills. Developing Wrestling Champions is the most complete guide to a successful wrestling program ever produced.

Technique presented includes high-percentage moves for all experience levels. Hundreds of action photos enable the reader to easily understand each step of every move. Daniel also includes the secrets and tips he learned en route to a coaching dual career record of 411-12-3 and nine Georgia State Championships.

Coaches at any level, athletic administrators, parents and boosters will also benefit from information on administering competition, increasing attendance, fund raising, producing a team publication, safety, using the media and dealing with officials.

A special feature for coaches is 'Daniel's Dozen', a discussion of twelve Absolute Truths that will enable them to avoid many conflicts and guide them through the awesome task of developing wrestling champions.

CONTENTS

CHAPTER 1

Let's Talk Philosophy

"Would you tell me please which way I ought to walk from here?" "That depends a good deal on where you want to get to," said the Cat. "I don't much care where", said Alice. "Then it doesn't matter which way you walk" said the Cat.
From *Alice's Adventures In Wonderland*

I know what you're thinking, "Oh no!, not another philosophy lecture. I got enough of those in college during education courses." Originally, I felt the same way, but soon realized that our philosophy determines our decisions throughout our careers. It determines how we deal with athletes, parents, officials, and our peers. Our philosophy guides us through life and helps us reach our destination in the form of established goals.

If you just want to coach, and like Alice, it doesn't really matter where you want your team to get to, your philosophy doesn't matter. You'll be like a sailboat without a sail wandering aimlessly through life with no team or career goals in sight.

Developing a sound philosophy depends on your values, standards, experiences, morals, and goals. I would never attempt to tell a coach what his philosophy should be, but will say "Develop your own or someone will develop it for you". Set your standards high and work to achieve them. Based on my experiences as a small town, church-going, country boy who was taught to always do the right thing, I developed a philosophy that has helped me reach many of my career goals. Not only was I able to be successful in wrestling as an athlete and coach, but also successful in the classroom as a student and a teacher.

My philosophy today consists of what I call 'Daniel's Dozen', twelve points or beliefs that I found useful in coaching, teaching, and dealing with peers.

DANIEL'S DOZEN

1. Wrestlers are a unique breed and the toughest of all athletes.

   The daily rugged practice routine, the 'blood, sweat, and tears', combined with the relentless issues of diet and weight control make the wrestler a 'different breed of animal'. The bonds formed in the sport of wrestling last a lifetime and are some of the stronger bonds in athletics.

2. It is an injustice to not push your athletes to achieve their maximum success.

Athletes have 'one shot' at a middle school career, 'one shot' at a high school career, and some get 'one shot' at a college career. A coach at any level that allows a wrestler to get by with less than his best is doing a great injustice to the athlete, his parents, the team, and the school. Demand their best, accept no less! The U.S. Army's old slogan, "Be all you can be!" is very applicable to wrestlers.

I realize that a few athletes are self-motivators and are able to push themselves to a point, but when fatigue rears its' ugly head, it's time for the coach to step in and take them to the next level physically, mentally, and emotionally. It is unrealistic for a coach to expect an athlete to perform successfully in a zone he's never experienced. You've got to get them there by making practice tougher than any match could ever be. By doing this, they develop confidence in your philosophy, your technique, and your ability to conditioning athletes. Remember: "Work will, wishing won't"

3. The mind tires much more quickly than the body does.

While the body continues to work hard, the mind begins to weaken. Wrestlers often tell themselves, "I'm so tired, I can't go anymore". They begin to focus on little strains, bruises, and bumps and begin to feel sorry for themselves.

I've always found it amusing that a kid with an injured finger constantly focuses on it. Though the other 99.9% of his body feels fine, the 0.1% commands all his attention.

When wrestlers tell me they are totally exhausted, I explain to them that they really don't understand fatigue. Fatigue is carrying over 100 pounds of gear in 120 degree temperatures in Iraq for months; fatigue is running a 26 mile marathon in 100 degree weather; fatigue is a mom working 80 hours a week to make a living for her children.

"You are just temporarily out of energy", I explain. They usually seem to get the point.

I also explain that their fatigue is basically a lack of motivation. "If I placed $1,000,000 cash five miles down the road and it could be yours if you run get it now, could you do it?", I ask. The obvious answer is "Yes". "See, I say, it's a matter of motivation". It might be a lame story, but the message is there. No matter how far you've pushed yourself, you can always go a little farther.

As a final way to explain that they often place limits on themselves, I do the following. On a practice day, when the guys seem to be 'dragging around', I stop practice. I have all the guys sit in front of me, in a semi-circle. I ask them to raise their right hand in the air as far as they can. I pause, and then say "Now, raise it an inch farther". They all do, which proves my point. When we think we've pushed ourselves to the maximum, we can always push a little harder.

4. Kids don't care how much you know until they know how much you care.

    It is important for a coach to know 'a lot of stuff', but it is more important that he genuinely cares for his athletes as individuals. Always take time to talk with them if only for a couple of minutes. Try to find something positive to say each day, if it's only "Nice job", "Awesome takedown", "Good hustle", "Way to work".

    When my six year old son, Dusty would come home from T-ball practice, I'd always ask "How was practice, Big Man?" He would sometimes say "Great". When I asked why it was great, his typical response was, "Coach said I did a good job hitting today". Those few kind words, "You did a good job hitting", made all the difference in the world to him coming from his coach.

    Believe it or not, kids can sense how you feel about them as athletes and people in general.

    It is important to know and care about their home life, their friends, their problems, and their goals. There's a thin line between being interested and being nosey, so tread carefully. Work hard to be a demanding, but caring and supportive coach, who always keeps what's best for his athletes in mind.

5. A great coach never stops learning.

    We all have our basic philosophy, practice plan, off-season program, techniques, and drills.

    It is important to never think you know it all, regardless of how much you win or have won. Learning to coach is a never-ending process even if it is only a new setup, a new drill, a new move, a new teaching technique, a promotion idea, a match strategy, a fund-raising idea, or a way to deal with a problem. When I attend clinics and camps, I am basically looking for one or two new things that would fit into my program. Any coach that tries to change his total program depending on the camp he attends each summer is doomed to fail. We all do basically the same big things, but it's the 'little things' that separate coaches.

    Read professional periodicals, watch technique videos and DVDs, listen to other coaches, go to camps and clinics, read books and learn from the Masters who have come before you.

6. He who has not given everything has given nothing.

    This means the coach and the athlete. The coach must always be prepared mentally and physically for the practices, meets, and tournaments. He must be a good record keeper, good organizer, great communicator, and good planner. He must strive to learn more each season and continue to improve. Off-season work must be planned, organized, and supervised by the coach when possible. Remember: Coaches don't plan to fail, they just fail to plan!

    We had a t-shirt back in the 80's that summed up our expectations for the wrestlers. It simply said "ALL IT TAKES IS ALL YOU GOT".

7. The coach is a role model for all his athletes.

   For many kids, the father is the most important and stable role model they have. In today's society, however, coaches are taking on a much greater role in the lives of their wrestlers. Broken homes, dysfunctional families, and nuclear families are the cause of the change. Athletes often spend more time with their coach than with their families. Not only are they going to look to the coach for advice and guidance, they are carefully watching how you react in every situation whether it be positive or negative. It's an awesome responsibility and should be taken very seriously.

8. Change is inevitable.

   Successful coaches have the ability to adapt to the changing times. Just because it has always worked doesn't insure that it always will. A coach must be aware of changing technique, new weight control measures, and society's ever-changing attitude. In the 'old days' you could say to a kid, "Do it or else" and they'd do it. Today, you say "Do it or else" and some say "Let's hear a little about the else part".

   Though we must keep our basic philosophy and program in tact, flexibility is often very advantageous and can reap many benefits. We have heard repeatedly that the only constant is change. A coach, even a veteran, must be willing to make changes or be left in the past.

9. Athletes want and need structure and discipline.

   In the 21st Century, athletics are one of the last strongholds of discipline in our society. Productive athletes, as well as productive citizens, must have self-discipline, intensity, morals, positive self-esteem, and a sense of self-worth.

   A solid wrestling program provides all the opportunities and resources an athlete needs to develop into a good human being.

10. Negativity can destroy a wrestler, a wrestling team, and a wrestling program.

    Every coach and wrestler has a small voice inside their head that spouts negativity; "You can't", "It is not possible", "Don't go to practice", "Do it later", "It's not worth it", "I don't have the time", "We can't", "Nobody cares", "It'll never work" . . . and on and on and on! This negativity will destroy you, your wrestlers, or even your total program if you allow it to do so.

    What you think and say to yourself shapes your attitude. Negative self-talk most often leads to negative feelings, a negative attitude, and poor performance. Positive self-talk and feelings are most often associated with a good attitude, good performances, and the satisfaction of accomplishment.

    Even though it is often very difficult, remain positive. The old saying about making lemonade when life gives you lemons has credibility. Block out the negative thoughts and replace them with positive thoughts and phrases. I'm sure we've all heard the saying, "If you think you can or can't, you're probably right".

I've always stressed to my students and athletes, "We are Amer I CANS, not Amer I CAN'T's!"

11. You should expect jealousy, resentment, and criticism from some rivals and peers.

As our teenagers so eloquently state, "The world is full of haters." They want nothing more than to see you fail. In a perfect society, we would all rejoice at our peers' accomplishments and praise them for their hard work and achievement. Unfortunately, in today's society many resent those who work hard and achieve lofty goals, especially peers, rivals, and fellow coaches who are involved in losing programs. I decided early in my career to let the jealousy and resentment toward me act as the wind against a kite and push me to even higher levels of success.

12. You should never look back with regret.

We all make decisions that we sometimes regret. I believe that it is a mistake to look back and begin the coulda, shoulda, woulda self-talk. Make the best decision you can, at that time, with the information you have and move on. Don't worry about the past, look to the future. Worry does not help tomorrow it only takes away from today.

These twelve points and beliefs have enabled me to have a successful career. I don't expect everyone to adopt all the points, but hopefully, they will serve as a stimulus to make you take a long look at what you actually believe in and want to do in your program and life. Regardless of the philosophy you adopt, be yourself at all times. As the beautiful singer-actress Judy Garland said, "Always be a first-rate version of your self, instead of a second-rate version of someone else."

CHAPTER 2

Basics, Basics, and More Basics

Successful wrestling coaches traditionally develop their programs around the Seven Basic Skills of wrestling. They include stance, motion, level change, penetration, back-step, back-arch, and lift. In addition to the previous seven skills, add an eighth called 'torque'. Torque is the 'rotational force' applied to an object. In several wrestling techniques, rotational force is necessary for success and torque must be added to the list.

Of the basic skills in wrestling, stance seems to be the most underrated, underappreciated and least emphasized. I consider stance the most important skill. Some would disagree, I'm sure, but here's my logic. The stance is the foundation for all technique, both offensive and defensive. Regardless of how awesome your Duckunder, Fireman's Carry, Snapdown, Heel Pick and Headlock are, they will never be used to their maximum from a poor stance. A great stance is the foundation for all technique. It is comparable to having a solid foundation for skyscrapers. Regardless of what is put on top, or added, it is worthless without a good foundation.

Stance

(2:1)

There are two basic types of stances; square and staggered. The square stance (2:1) is primarily used for lateral movement as in setups, while the staggered stance is used for penetration. The appropriate position for a square stance has the knees slightly bent, head up, feet shoulder width apart, elbows in beside the ribs, and one's weight evenly distributed on the balls of the feet. The shoulders, knees, and toes should be vertically aligned maintaining a good center of gravity.(2:2) The palms should face downward with the hands open, fingers slightly spread, and relaxed for quicker movements. Tensing of the arms and hands causes early fatigue and should be avoided.

(2:2)   **(2:3)**

The staggered or penetration stance (2:3) is basically the same as the square stance with the exception of having one foot dropped back and one's level lowered. The foot may be pointed forward or turned sideways for a broader pushing surface.

Drills For Stance and Motion Development

Daily drill on stance is imperative for maximum success. Several simple drills have been designed to develop an effective stance.

The Slide Drill is a basic technique for developing the square stance. On the coach's whistle, the wrestlers break down into a stance. On the second whistle, they move in one direction, stop, and move in the opposite direction. They slide their feet on the mat as opposed to picking them up as in a hopping movement.

Each quick movement should only cover four or five inches. The front foot always moves first (the foot that is in the direction you are moving), then the trail foot. To develop the concept of one foot pulling the other, it is beneficial to visualize a strong rubber band connecting the ankles. One moves slightly then pulls the other the exact same distance. Wrestlers should move slowly at first (under control) making frequent direction changes. As they feel more comfortable, they should increase their quickness of movement. It is important to avoid moving in a pattern as in left, left, left, right, right, right, left, left, left) Advanced wrestlers will notice an opponent's patterns and time their shots (takedowns attempts) accordingly.

Mirror Drill

An excellent exercise to develop the square stance is the Mirror Drill. With two wrestlers facing each other, one becomes the mover and the other is the mirror. The object of the drill is for Wrestler A to move in lateral directions with frequent changes while Wrestler B 'mirrors' his movements. This drill teaches Wrestler A to move while maintaining a good stance, while B learns to react to A's movements and stay square (facing) at all times. Alternating 20-30 second spurts is very effective. As the wrestlers mature, level changes and fakes may be added to create a more realistic situation.

Freeze Drill

(2:4)

The Freeze Drill is used to develop the ability to maintain a good stance during drills and competition. Wrestler A 'freezes' and remains in a square stance. Wrestler B then grabs (hooks) the head of A and begins to move him by pushing, pulling, snapping, and circling in an effort to get him out of his stance. (2:4) A's only role is to maintain a proper stance with his neck firmly bowed with his head up. On the coach's command, wrestlers switch roles. It is important to note that both wrestlers should maintain a proper stance at all times, as there is a tendency for the wrestler that is pushing and pulling to lose his position. Alternating 20-30 second spurts is most effective.

Wall Drill

(2:5)

The Wall Drill is used to develop proper movement from the stance position as well as endurance and power. Wrestlers line up and begin to move laterally along a wall (longest in room) in their stance with their knees bent in an exaggerated position (2:5). This drill provides an excellent opportunity for the coach to examine foot position and movement. Wrestlers should move along the wall to the end then jog back to the front of the line. After a few minutes, they should change directions.

Tennis Ball Drill

(2:6)

(2:7)

Tennis balls placed between the elbows and sides are excellent for teaching wrestlers to keep their elbows in while moving in a stance (2:6). Most tennis coaches are willing to donate old balls if asked to do so. This drill is extremely important for new and younger wrestlers as it develop muscle memory.

The balls may also be used while performing the Freeze Drill and Mirror Drill. (2:7)

Quick Feet-Pitter Patter

The purpose of the Quick Feet / Pitter Patter Drill is two-fold. First, it is to develop quickness in moving the feet in a stance. Secondly, it is excellent for conditioning at the end of practice to develop endurance in the power center. The position of the wrestlers is the same as on the Wall Drill. On command, wrestlers become very light on their feet and chop them rapidly as possible in short spurts. It is important to listen for the quick pitter-patter sound of landing on the balls of the feet as opposed to hearing a stomping noise resulting from landing flat-footed. Alternating fifteen second spurts of movement with five seconds of rest is effective.

Butt Kickers-Knee Ups

(2:8)   **(2:9)**

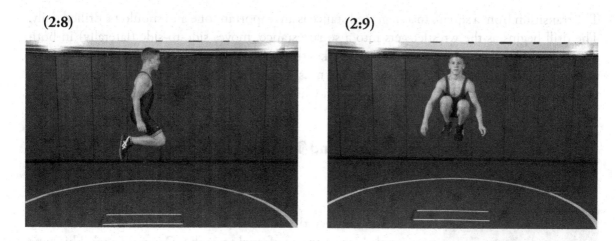

To develop power in the hips and thighs, Butt Kickers and Knee Ups may be incorporated into daily practices. Repetitions may be done in groups of 20-20, 10-10, 5-5, or alternately 1-1, 1-1, 1-1. In Butt-Kickers, the wrestler jumps directly up and tries to kick himself in the buttocks (2:8) with the bottoms of his feet. The Knee Ups require the wrestler to jump up and pull his knees to his chest (2:9). This is another excellent drill to develop power and strength in the hip and thigh area-the wrestler's power center.

Staggered or Penetration Stance

The staggered stance is frequently referred to as the penetration stance. Its primary purpose is to move forward to attack one's opponent as opposed to the square stance which is basically for set ups. The position is basically the same as the square stance, with the exception of the staggered leg and the lowering of the wrestler's hips. To transition from square to staggered, one must simply lower his level by bending the knees and dropping one foot back from which to push-off. The staggered foot may be almost aligned with the lead foot or turned sideways for a better push-off surface. The bent trail leg may be visualized as a coiled spring ready to propel the wrestler forward into and through his opponent. Level changes are created by bending the knees only. Bending of the back is unacceptable.

Jab Step

The jab step is a short step taken by pushing forward off the back foot. It is only a six to eight inch step, but enough to make a difference on penetration success.

To develop the Jab Step, simply push off the back coiled leg, and step the lead foot forward six to eight inches along the mat. Be careful to immediately bring the trail leg forward the same distance. The lead foot must stay close to the mat rather than taking a high step.

Transition Drill

The transition from a square to a staggered stance is an important one and should be drilled daily. The drill begins as the wrestler gets into a square stance, moves side-to-side (laterally) in both directions. He then drops one foot back and takes three or four jab steps forward. He then returns to a square stance and repeats the process. He must remember to lower his level when dropping the foot back, keep his head up and elbows in, while visualizing the coiled spring in his leg.

The Danger Zone and The Daniel Triangle

(2:10)

The area between the wrestler's feet and extending back to form a triangle is commonly referred to as the 'Danger Zone'. This zone must be penetrated by the offensive wrestler to execute almost all takedowns. The penetration may be by a hand, foot, hip, head, or leg.

The Daniel Triangle (2:10) is an effective way to get beginners to visualize the 'Danger Zone' and realize the importance of the jab step and drop step in penetration.

(2:11)   **(2:12)**

Equilateral triangles are placed on the mat using two inch athletic tape. The tape should then be covered with mat tape to prevent the athletic tape from rolling up or moving. Each side of the triangle should be between twelve and sixteen inches long. Coaches may wish to make various size triangles depending on the team's size range.

One wrestler places his heels on two angles with the triangle extending behind him. At bent arms length, the offensive wrestler takes a jab step and drop steps his knee into the (Danger Zone) triangle (2:11). He grasps the opponent's legs behind both knees or wraps the calves (2:12) He then steps up with his trail leg, releases his grip, stands, and returns to a staggered stance.

The Drop Step Drills and Penetration

The Drop Step, or penetration step is used to enter the opponent's Danger Zone and can only be executed from a staggered stance. After the jab step has been taken, the wrestler drops forward to his lead leg knee being careful to keep his elbows in and head up. The trail leg knee stays off the mat, and steps up after the front knee touches the mat. Lowering the hips helps avoid pounding the front knee on the mat.

Penetration, penetration, penetration! No penetration equals failure. It is beneficial during practice to bring a wrestler to the front of the team. Holding a piece of chalk or similar object in your fingers, tell the team it is a bullet. "It's a bullet traveling 100 miles per hour", you tell them as you move it toward Tommy's chest. As it hits his chest, drop it to the floor). Then you ask why Tommy was not injured. The obvious answer is, "NO PENETRATION". Explain that it's the same with wrestling takedowns; the absence of penetration equals failure.

The Duck Walk

(2:13)

A lead up drill for the drop step is the Duck Walk. The wrestler kneels on one knee (as on Picture Day) and places his hands on his belly-button (2:13). He drops forward to his front knee and steps up with his back foot. He then drops to his other knee and steps up with his other foot. Many coaches do this drill daily as a sports-specific warm up exercise. It loosens the groin area, hips, thighs, and hamstrings while emphasizing proper technique. Carefully monitor the trail leg to insure it stays off the mat. Keeping the hands on the bellybutton helps develop balance while in the position. As balance and competency increase, direct the wrestlers to reach forward, grasp an imaginary leg or legs, and pull it (or them) toward the chest with each stride. Improvements in timing will come fairly quickly with daily repetitions. The hands should be as far apart as the object they are grasping; six to eight inches for a single leg, 18-24 inches for double legs.

Casper Drill

(2:14)

Prior to teaching the Casper Drill, a good teaching technique is to have a second wrestler stand behind the first wrestler before the drill begins. Explain to the wrestlers that they are to visualize penetrating to take Casper (the Ghost) down. (2:14)

This drill requires a partner who is in a square stance. The wrestler moves to a bent arms length from his partner in a staggered stance. He takes a jab step and drop steps into the danger zone. As the offensive wrestler shoots, the defensive wrestler slowly walks backward. This action simulates a defensive wrestler moving backward as if to sprawl. Once the offensive wrestler grasps behind the opponent's knees (with his chest and head up), he steps forward with his trail leg and returns to a staggered stance. He repeats the drill by moving to a staggered stance, jab stepping and drop stepping across the mat. REMEMBER: In the beginning, it's not how fast drills are executed that count, but how correctly they are performed.

Benefits of the Daniel Triangle

The benefits of using the Daniel Triangle are:

1. It is beneficial for all skill levels.

2. It helps wrestlers visualize the danger zone which carries over to matches.

3. It makes it easy for the coach to evaluate proper penetration technique.

4. It keeps wrestlers in their practice area.

5. It develops the basic skills of level-change and penetration.

6. It enables wrestlers to do self-evaluation on penetration

Over And Under Drill

(2:15)

(2:16)

(2:17)

The Over and Under Drill is a warm up and conditioning drill. It may be done in pairs or as a team. The pair drill begins with both wrestlers in a stance (2:15). The defensive wrestler is in a square stance; the offensive wrestler is in a staggered stance. The offensive wrestler drop steps, penetrating between the wrestler's legs (2:16). He stands and 'leap frogs' over his partner (2:17), then quickly repeats the procedure. It is permissible to place both hands on the mat to help propel yourself through your partner's leg. After the offensive wrestler penetrates, stands and turns, the defensive wrestlers bends over and places his elbows on his knees enabling the leap frog.

The group drill is the same technique, but has a slightly different format. All the wrestlers are positioned in a large circle approximately six to eight feet apart with their elbows on knees. A designated wrestler begins the drill by 'leap-frogging' over the first wrestler and 'drop-stepping' through the legs of the other, until the end of the circle. After the first wrestler leaps over the first wrestler and through the legs of the second, the next wrestler in line starts. The pattern continues until each guy reaches the end of the line where he awaits his turn to go again.

Dariel W. Daniel

Locking The Hands-A Small Detail With Great Consequences

(2:18)

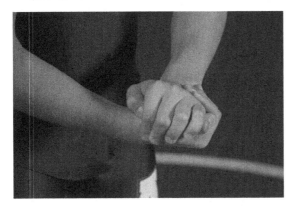

(2:19)

Locking the hands properly is a small detail with tremendous benefits. There are numerous ways to lock hands including the interlacing lock, the wrist lock, the fingers lock, thumb lock, and the pinkie lock. Of all the aforementioned, the thumb lock and pinkie lock are the more secure and most beneficial for strength and power. The reasoning is the locks allow you to pull inward (toward the chest) as well as pulling the elbows together and downward in a squeezing motion.

The Thumb Lock is performed by grasping the opposing thumb with the four fingers of the opposite hand. The 'pinkie finger' fits into the groove of the top wrist and your thumb fits into the groove on the bottom wrist (2:18). Beginners may learn the lock better by placing the hands in a 'praying position' and rotating the bottom 90 degrees. Of course, the 'praying position' and rotation is just a teaching aid, but with repeated repetitions, it soon becomes an automatic lock.

The pinkie lock, developed by the Russians, is almost the same as the thumb lock except the thumb grasps the pinkie on the rotating hand. (2:19) Obviously, the 'praying position' technique is only a lead up teaching technique as wrestlers will soon be able to master both the thumb and pinkie locks. These locks are appropriate for almost every locked hands situation you will encounter.

Tieups (Ties)

There are numerous tieups and each has a specific purpose, certain advantages, and certain disadvantages. Included are: Head and Elbow (often called the Collar Tie), Head and Biceps, Double Biceps, Underhook, Overhook, Russian Tie, Over and Under, and the Double Wrist Tie. All tie ups must be executed with correct head position and an appropriate stance. Though many of the quicker guys like to attempt takedowns from the outside without a tie up, ties allow one to control his opponent better, as well as get closer for a more high-percentage attack.

Head and Elbow (Collar Tie)

(2:20)

The Head and Elbow tie up is probably the oldest in modern history and least versatile for using technique. The primary uses of tying up this way are to stall to protect a lead, prevent a major decision, or avoid a technical fall. In the Head and Elbow, each wrestler neutralizes the other as they both have the exact same position (2:20). Wrestlers are usually in square stances, but the choice of stance has little impact in this position.

In the Head and Elbow tie up, the back of the opponents head is hooked (a hook is formed by cupping the hand and wrist around the neck) with your elbow down. The other hand (palm up) grasps the opponent's elbow with the index and middle fingers squeezing the elbow joint. The object is to 'hold on' while the time runs out.

Head and Biceps

(2:21)

The Head and Biceps tie is identical to the head and elbow, with the exception of the hand on the elbow. Cupping, or hooking, the head is critical in this tie. The hand is now placed on the inside of the biceps with the thumb in front of or the thumb behind the biceps. The thumb in front is sometimes used as a blocking, or defensive mechanism, while the thumb and four fingers behind the biceps (2:21) is used to pull the opponent forward to set up for takedowns.

Double Biceps

(2:22)

The Double Biceps is appropriately named. The offensive wrestler grasps the inside of both his opponent's arms (2:22) with his thumbs and fingers in a cupping position, around the biceps. The elbows must remain down as the forearms are the first line of defense if the opponent attempts a takedown. Some coaches may prefer to keep the thumbs on the insides of the arms.

Underhook

(2:23)   **(2:24)**

The Underhook is a very productive weapon for two reasons. First, it allows you to get closer to your opponent in a position of advantage. Secondly, many wrestlers are uncomfortable in an under hooked position and have few if any counters or defensive strategies. Underhooks are extremely practical and beneficial for heavyweights.

To secure the Underhook, club (snap the head forward with a cupped hand) the opponent and slide the opposite hand under the near arm and grabs defensive man's shoulder (2:23). A little force can assure that you secure the position.

Your elbow must be kept close to the opponent's body for more control and to prevent injury to oneself. In conjunction with the underhook, the opposite hand must control the opponent's head, biceps, or wrist. Inside head position makes the Underhook Tieup tighter and is used to block the opponent's attack (2:24).

Overhook Tieup

(2:25)   **(2:26)**

(2:27)   **(2:28)**

The Overhook Tieup possesses the same advantages as the Underhook Tieup. The only difference between the two is the arm goes over the opponent's biceps/triceps region rather than underneath it. (2:25)

The ability to change your opponent's head position is a must if you are to be successful with underhooks and overhooks. If the opponent has inside head position, take your free hand, cup his head (2:26), and pull it out in a 'swimming motion'. Slide the top of your head to the inside of his neck (2:27) obtaining the Overhook Tieup position (2:28).

Russian Tieup

(2:29)   **(2:30)**

The Russian Tieup has grown in popularity over the last decade and is frequently used in scholastic, freestyle and Greco-Roman matches. It is very effective on those who do not use it themselves or even drill with partners who do. There are a couple of simple ways to get into the Russian Tieup. The first is off the opponent's Head Tieup. First, turn your shoulder inward while tilting your head backward slightly to trap the wrist. With the opposite hand, firmly grab his wrist, still controlling the elbow (2:29) Next, pull his wrist toward your chest, holding it firmly. Release your grip on his elbow, hook his biceps, and pull it your chest.

The second way involves more quickness and force and is performed in an open stance (no tie up). Grab the wrist with the opposite hand, pull it toward the body and grab his biceps (palm up), and pull it against your chest (2:30). The grip on the wrist may be changed to have the palm facing upward.

Over And Under Tieup

(2:31)   **(2:32)**

The Over and Under Tieup results in each wrestler having his opponent's arm overhooked on one side and a type of underhook on the other side.(2:31) The head must be on the same side as the overhooked arm. Note: Both wrestlers are in the exact same position with the same opportunities to score. Some wrestlers elect to over hook the opponents arm holding it between their forearm and biceps. This technique makes it difficult to hold a sweaty wrestler. Grasping the opponents triceps/biceps area with the hand, curling the wrist around his upper arm, and clamping the arm to one's side creates three sources of control and has proven to be substantially more effective. (2:32) A basic lead up drill for beginners begins with each wrestler standing tall with both arms extended laterally and parallel to the mat. Then, both tilt their right arm downward 45 degrees as their left raises 45 degrees. They then move into the appropriate position get in a proper stance. The over hooked arm is used to pull the opponent around as a setup. The under hook is used to pull in the opposite direction as well to lift the opponents shoulder forcing the wrestler to shift his weight.

Double Wrist Tie

(2:33)

This tie involves grabbing both wrists, with the thumbs toward the inside. It requires quickness and a good, strong grip. (2:33) The hands may be on top of or beneath the wrists.

Double Underhook

(2:34)

To secure a Double Underhook, first secure a Single Underhook. Next, pommel or 'swim' the other hand to an inside position, and grab the shoulder as previously described. Immediately raise both arms until they are parallel to the mat. (2:34).

Overhook and Far Wrist Tieup

(2:35)

A variety of moves can be executed from a unique tie called the Overhook and Far Wrist. It places the opponent in a very awkward position where he has absolutely no control. After securing the overhook position, grasp the opponent's far wrist. (2:35) With a quick move, jerk his elbow toward your hand by pulling your wrist toward your outside hip. Grab his elbow, and pull both arms underneath your armpit tightly. He is now 'at your mercy'. Three options from this position are presented in Chapter 9.

CHAPTER 3

Takedowns: The King of Technique

Philosophy of Takedowns

Takedowns rule the wrestling world. If you can take someone down, the odds are in your favor to win the match. There are varying statistics on the correlation of getting the first takedown and winning the match. I've seen statistics stating that the guy who gets the first takedown wins between 70-80% of the time. Regardless of the exact number, the superior wrestler on his feet (neutral) has a definite advantage. One advantage is built into the rules as a wrestler has a chance to make two of the periods start in the neutral position every match.

It is my opinion that at least 80% of practice every day should be dedicated to drilling and wrestling in the neutral position. Some have argued that 80% is a disproportionate amount of time considering all the various techniques that must be covered during each practice. "That's only your opinion", they say. I always reply, "Yes, it is only my opinion, but it's one I value very highly". I contribute most of the success of my wrestlers to their takedown superiority.

We've all seen a wrestler secure a takedown within the first thirty seconds of a match, try to ride the guy (with his coach's blessing), only to get reversed in the last few seconds of the period. Though it makes absolutely no sense, it is a frequent occurrence in youth and high school wrestling. Superiority on your feet should be used to dominate your opponent.

10 Reasons A Coach Should Emphasize Takedowns

EVERY Practice EVERY Day EVERY Year

1. Wrestlers can make two of the three periods begin in the neutral position.

2. Two points are greater than one, so the take 'em down and let 'em go philosophy makes sense mathematically.

3. Six minutes on the feet is longer than six minutes on the mat. Only superior-conditioned athletes can wrestle on their feet for six minutes.

4. Superiority on the feet can demoralize the opponent by the repeated takedown and release method.

5. Many wrestlers can be thrown or taken to their back by takedowns that cannot be turned from the top position.

6. The first period in overtime begins in the neutral position.

7. With the ability to throw (headlocks, lateral drops, arm spins) the wrestler is never 'out of the match'.

8. Superiority on the feet is a real confidence builder.

9. Superiority on the feet allows wrestlers to take away the greatest weapon of Granby Roll teams by using the optional start.

10. It is easier to get a stalling call in the neutral position with an aggressive attack.

Nothing in wrestling is more exciting, interesting, and crowd pleasing than watching a highly skilled wrestler on his feet. With precision setups and technique, he takes his opponent down with seemingly little effort. It's the finished product of thousands of hours of drill on display and a pleasure to watch. Statistics have shown over the years that single and double leg attacks are the most successful takedowns on every level of competition. They must be a part of every wrestler's technique if he is to succeed on any level. Also considered to be basic takedowns are the Duck Under, Hi Crotch, Front Headlock, Snap Down, Arm Drag, Fireman's (Carry /Roll/Outside), Snap Drag, Elbow Shuck, Wrist Trap, Lateral Drop, Hip Toss, Headlock and variations of each. You must also develop takedowns off your opponent's attempts to take you down.

By now you should be familiar with the basic skills of proper stance, motion, tieups, level changes, drop step and penetration. All are necessary for success in the realm of takedowns.

Double Leg Takedowns

In the old days, the Double Leg was called a Double Leg Tackle (undoubtedly a reference to football). It progressed to a Double Leg Dive, and now is simply referred to as a Regular Double or simply, a Double. As the name implies, the offensive wrestler attacks both legs of his opponent. Variations of the Double Leg are the Flair Double and the Blast Double.

Regular Double

Tie Up or Position (Head/Biceps, Double Biceps, Double Wrist, Open)

(3:1)

(3:2)

(3:3)

The key to a successful double is to get the lead foot in line with the opponent's crotch. This enables a quick jab step, drop step, and an explosive takedown. If the opponent is in a staggered stance, a side step and quick jerk on his head, biceps, or wrist is necessary to make him step forward into a square stance. A Double Leg on an opponent in a staggered stance without a tie is not practical or possible. A Regular Double consists of the setup, jab step, lowering one's level, a drop step (3:1), grabbing both knees and follow through to the mat. (3:2) Three options are available when grabbing both legs. Some prefer to grab each leg behind the knee, some prefer to wrap or snake the calves, while other try to lock their hands around both legs. The offensive wrestler should pull his legs forward, sink his hips and spread his knees for maximum control after the takedown. (3:3)

Blast Double

Tie Up or Position (Head/Biceps, Double Biceps, Double Wrist, Open)

(3:4)

(3:5)

(3:6)

The Blast Double Leg setup, foot position and jab step are exactly like the Regular Double. The only differences are the level change and the head position. In a Blast Double, the level change is less and only enough to place your forehead in the opponent's sternum and grab his hamstrings (3:4). Keep your head up and your neck bowed

Driving forward, the hamstrings of the opponent are held tightly and he is power-driven to the mat (3:5). The offensive wrestler should scoot his knees forward, sink his hips, and spread his knees for maximum control after the takedown (3:6)

Flair Double

Tie Up or Position (Head / Biceps, Double Biceps, Double Wrist, Open)

(3:7)

A slight variation of the Regular Double, the Flair Double has grown rapidly in popularity. The major difference between the two is that with the Flair Double you step up with his outside foot, push your opponent's body with his head causing his weight to shift to the opposite foot. Lift his near leg, chop his far leg at the knee (3:7) and dump him to the mat gaining control.

Finishes When Your Opponent Sprawls

Eventually, every wrestler gets caught 'underneath' his opponent. Usually the opponent has sprawled to stop a single, double, or a fireman's carry. Though it is one of the tougher situations from which to recover, there are several excellent moves proven to be successful.

Iranian Series (Back Door Series)

(3:8)

(3:9)

(3:10)

The Iranian or 'back door' Series is one of the better packages because of the many options available. Moves are included if the defensive wrestler grabs your ankles or locks around the waist as well as from a regular sprawl.

In all the Iranian Series moves, it is imperative that you establish a base from which to operate. First, secure a tight grip around either leg (3:8). Next, frog-hop your knees forward and under your chest. Hold the leg with one hand, and place your other hand on the mat directly under your shoulder (3:9). Push off your hand and step your leg up to a 90 degree angle as on Picture Day. (3:10) Note: If your opponent grabs your ankles, you will not be able to step up.

Back Door

(3:11)

To complete the Back Door, relax your grip on the opponent's thigh slightly, reach over the controlled leg (hamstrings) with your opposite arm and drop to both knees as you pivot to face in the opposite direction. (3:11)

Turtle

(3:12)   **(3:13)**

(3:14)   **(3:15)**

The Turtle move involves holding onto the leg with one hand, placing the other palm on the opposite thigh (3:12). The head is pulled down and shoulders moved up (as a turtle pulling his head into his shell). Pull down on the leg and push up (and over) on the thigh (3:13) forcing him to the mat. (3:14). It is critical to stay up and cover the opponent after he has hit the mat. (3:15)

Heel Pull

(3:16)

(3:17)

(3:18)

Using the leg as a lever, grab his heel securely and lock the knee. (3:16) Pull the heel quickly over the opposite knee as you duck your head. (3:17) Keep the leg extended (locked) throughout the move. Cover your opponent as he hits the mat.(3:18)

Heel Pull With Your Ankles Grabbed

(3:19)

(3:20)

When the opponent grabs your ankles (3:19) the action is the same as the heel pull, except your knee is not up. As you pull downward on the heel, kick your opposite leg back as far as possible.

(3:20) Due to the powerful pull on the heel and forceful leg extension, the defensive wrestler is unable to hold on to the ankle and falls to his side. Cover him as soon as he hits the mat.

Finish When Opponent Locks Hands Around Waist

(3:21)

(3:22)

(3:23)

(3:24)

(3:25)

Often the defensive wrestler knows he is in trouble and locks his hands around your waist. (3:21) This is the only time in the series that going to your side is permissible.

Hold on to both legs tightly. Fall to either side (3:22) Hook his bottom leg and hold it securely. (3:23) Using your top hand to push the top thigh away (3:24) and free your head. Turn and cover him to secure a takedown. (3:25)

Tripod Walk-Chase Ankle

(3:26)

(3:27)

On some occasions, the Tripod Walk is available. After the frog hop, place both hands on the mat (one on top of the other), extend your arms and raise your butt in the air (3:26). Walk around toward his ankle while keeping your hands posted. Use your top hand to grab his near ankle and pull it upward.(3:27) Extending your arms and raising your hips decreases the defensive wrestler's angles and his ability to execute a Whizzer or Hiplock.

Peek Out

(3:28)

(3:29)

The Peek Out comes when the defensive wrestler is draped over you with his hands around your waist. Slide the same side elbow out and back as you swim (peek) your head out (3:28). Your head and elbow push back on his arm and body as you slide around behind him for two points. (3:29)

The Peek-Out Drill

The Peek-Out Drill is exactly the same as the Peek Out move, EXCEPT after the offensive wrestlers scores, he spins around front and allows the other guy to peek out, spin around, and become the defensive wrestler.

Single Leg Takedowns and Finishes

Single leg takedowns are the most successful takedowns in the world at all levels of competition. Singles may be Sweep Single, Low Single, Snatch Single, and Outside Single. The Outside Single and Snatch Single consist of two parts; picking the leg up, and a second move to take the opponent down to the mat. The Sweep Single and Low Single take the wrestler directly to the mat and require no second move if correctly performed. The Snatch Single is considered primarily a heavyweight move. The Outside Single is the most popular of all single attacks.

Sweep Single

Tie Up or Position (Head/Biceps, Double Biceps, Double Wrist, Open, Underhook)

(3:30)   **(3:31)**

The Sweep Single is performed by making the opponent step forward by using the tie ups listed, or attacking the lead leg. Your strength in attacking both sides may be the determining factor in your strategy. Taking an outside step toward the leg to be attacked, drop to your back knee. (3:30) The head pushes laterally into his body above the hip (head up, back straight) laterally as the hands are Butterfly locked around the lower leg. Pushing laterally off your lead foot and head, the opponent is forced to shift his weight to the opposite leg.(3:31) His leg is pulled up in front or to the side of your body and one of the following actions is used to take him to the mat.

Front Trip

(3:32)

(3:33)

(3:34)

With the opponents leg in front of you (3:32), place your inside arm around his waist and grab his hip. Pulling up on his far hip to raise his weight off his foot (3:33), use your inside leg to trip your opponent above the knee taking him to the mat. (3:34) (Note: If your opponent has a Whizzer or Hiplock, 'limp arm' on the way to the mat by sliding the back of your hand across his leg.)

Back Trip

(3:35)

(3:36)

(3:37)   **(3:38)**

The Back Trip requires you to grab your opponent's near shoulder while holding his leg tightly (3:35).

Step across and block his far heel (3:36). Pull down on his shoulder and up on his leg simultaneously as you fall to your inside hip. (3:37)

Be sure to step up while maintaining control (3:38)

Foot Sweep

(3:39)   **(3:40)**   **(3:41)**

Executing the Foot Sweep requires you to pull up on the opponent's leg (3:39) and sweep his foot from underneath him (3:40). Remember to cover him as soon as he hits the mat. (3:41) (Note: Use your hand around your opponent's waist to shift his weight off the foot to be 'swept')

Tree Top

(3:42)

(3:43)

(3:44)

The Tree Top involves stepping away from your opponent laterally (3:42), pulling his foot as high 'as a tree top' while standing on your toes (3:43) and taking him to the mat (3:44). Remember! You are always responsible for your opponent's safe return to the mat!

Hop Back to a Double

(3:45)

(3:46)

(3:47)

My favorite finish is the 'Hop Back to a Double'. It is fundamentally sound and has proven to be very effective and hard to stop. After lowering your level, step back (3:45) making your opponent hop forward (3:46). As he posts his foot, drop step and grab his other leg. (3:47)

Thigh Pull

(3:48)   **(3:49)**

To execute the Thigh Pull, grab your opponent's thigh with your free hand. Reach under his leg with your arm and grab your own biceps. (3:48) Step back with your inside leg and pull down hard on the thigh, forcing your opponent to the mat. (3:49)

Leg Spin

(3:50)   **(3:51)**

(3:52)

The Leg Spin is very similar to the Underarm Spin and Jap Whizzer. The action is the same, but you spin under the opponent's leg rather than under his arm. It's a very effective technique, especially since few wrestlers or coaches are familiar with it. Holding the leg up, step forward and punch your fist under his knee (3:50). Arch and fall toward the mat to take him down. (3:51). Rotate to your stomach immediately after your head hits the mat.(3:52)

If his leg is between your legs.

Wrestlers who prefer to pick the single leg up often find themselves in a situation where the opponent's leg is leg is between their own legs. Two moves have proven to be very successful in this situation, the Low Double and the Heel Setback. Rarely seen in today's competition, both are very effective moves.

The Low Double

(3:53)   **(3:54)**

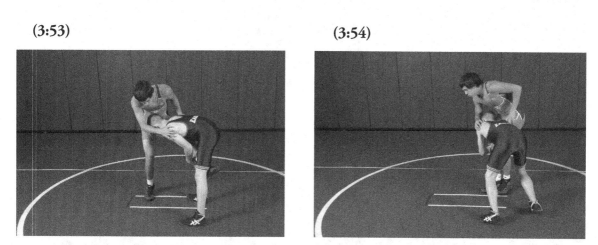

With a single leg trapped between your legs, face your opponent. Hold his leg securely by pressing your chest against his knee. With your front foot, step backwards quickly (3:53), and Drop Step into a Low Double Leg Takedown. (3:54)

Heel Setback

(3:55)   (3:56)

The Heel Setback is a move from the 70's and rarely seen today. It is, however, a very effective move when performed correctly. With the leg trapped between your legs, make sure his knee is locked out by your chest pressure. Reach back and grab the opponent's entire foot with your outside hand (3:55). Step laterally away from his leg, and push your head backwards into his thigh to take him down (3:56).

To get his leg from between your legs:

Some wrestlers prefer to have the opponent's leg out from between his own legs. Many wrestlers feel more 'in control' when the leg is out and in front of them. Two simple ways to 'get the leg out' are the Mule Kick and the Forward March.

Mule Kick

(3:57)   (3:58)

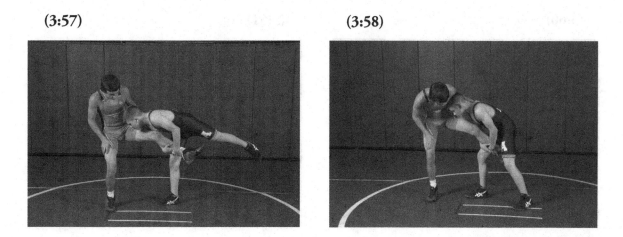

In the Mule Kick, simply kick your outside leg back parallel to the mat (3:57). As you kick, reach down and grab the opponent's lower leg, pull it up toward, (3:58) and then under your armpit and lock it tightly.

Forward March

(3:59)

With the leg locked out, as in the Mule Kick, simply march forward! When you step with your front leg (3:59), reach down and pull the leg up. Lock the ankle under the armpit.

If the leg is on the outside:

If your opponent has kept his leg on the outside and has a Whizzer in, you have three alternatives to take him down. They are the Leg Lift with a Back Trip; the Swing to Duckunder Lift; and the Knee Push / Inside Trip.

Leg Lift With Back A Trip

(3:60)

(3:61)

(3:62)

With the opponent's leg secured on the outside, reach around his waist with your forward hand (3:60), use your hip to lift him and get the weight off his foot. Step behind his leg (3:61) and trip him to the mat (3:62)

Swing to Duckunder Lift

(3:63)

(3:64)

(3:65)

(3:66)

With the opponent's leg securely held on the outside, use torque to swing him forward (3:63). Lower your level, duck under his armpit (between his body and the Whizzer arm) (3:64). Step forward and use your hips to lift him off the mat and onto your shoulder. Safely take him down (3:65) to his back and stay between his legs. (3:66)

Knee Push / Inside Leg Trip or Back Trip

(3:67)   **(3:68)**

With the opponent's leg tightly secured, take the palm of your other hand and push outward on the opponent's inner thigh (3:67), jerk his leg up (3:68) and under your armpit.

There are two options available from this position:

Inside Leg Trip

Take a step with your inside leg hooking the opponent's leg and tripping him to the mat. Be sure to spread your arms wide as you fall to establish a good base.

Back Trip

(3:69)   **(3:70)**

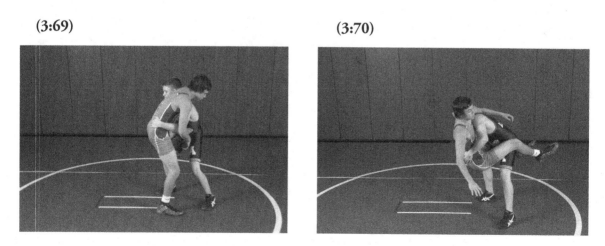

(3:71)

After the push-pull action, reach around his waist with your free arm (3:69), lift and back trip him (3:70) to the mat. (3:71)

Straight Low Single

(Open position with no tie up)

(3:72)

(3:73)

The Straight Low Single is very effective for those athletes with exceptional quickness. The Straight Low Single is often done 'right off the whistle' and is usually effective on an unprepared or tired wrestler with all his weight on his front foot. It is also very effective after a good setup which pulls his foot forward and posts it.

In a staggered stance with your level very low, take a small jab step followed by a quick lunge. Penetrating deep, place your shoulder on the opponent's shoelaces with your head on the inside (3:72). Grab his ankle with one or more hands and take him down. (3:73)

Low Outside Single

Tie Up or Position (Head and Biceps, Double Biceps, Double Wrists, Open Stance)

(3:74)

(3:75)

The Low Outside Single is a 'low-risk' move because it does not require you to go underneath your opponent. In the event he sprawls, you are not caught underneath him, but are able to simply go behind him for a takedown.

The primary key to making the Low Outside Single successful is proper foot position. Your foot must be aligned with the foot you plan to attack. It is often referred to as 'cheating' the foot over.

After moving your opponent around to where you have proper foot position, lower your level, drop step to the outside keeping your head low and near his foot (3:74). Pivot on your front knee as you grab his ankle with both arms, and jerk it back for a takedown. (3:75)

Snatch Single from an Underhook

Tie up or Position (Underhook)

(3:76)

(3:77)

(3:78)

From the under hook position, make sure your head is on the inside and your body is perpendicular to him (3:76). Raise you elbow (3:77) and quickly lower your level by bending your knees. Reach down, lock both hands around his knee and snatch the leg up. (3:78)

Use any of the second moves previously described to take him down from this position.

The Duckunder Series

The Duckunder Series requires the least amount of strength and energy of any takedown. It is a versatile move because it can be done from a variety of tieups, from both sides, and using varied set ups. It is usually most successful from the Double Biceps, Head and Biceps, Underhook, and Double Wrists ties. Depending on your skill and preferences, the Duckunder may take the opponent directly to the mat, or result in a 'go behind' situation requiring a second move to actually take him to the mat and gain control.

A couple of interesting set ups include pulling him toward you by both biceps as you duck (twice as quick) and pulling down on one biceps forcing him to react by pulling it back up.

Scarecrow Lead-up Drill to Develop a Duckunder

(3:79)

(3:80)

(3:81)

The Duckunder is a fairly difficult move to teach. The Scarecrow lead-up drill has proven to be an excellent tool in helping athletes to understand and develop the concept of lowering their level, pivoting, and pushing with their head.

In a square stance, the defensive wrestler lowers his level and holds both arms out in a scarecrow-like position (3:79). The offensive wrestler cheats his foot forward to the Duckunder side and lowers his level, steps forward placing his head under the opponent's armpit and on his back (3:80), pivots (torques) and pushes his partner forward with his head (3:81)

The offensive wrestler does NOT tie up or use his hands. This places all the emphasis on the torque motion using the hips and head. For purposes of the drill, the coach may require the offensive wrestler to lock his hands behind his own back.

The Basic Duckunder

Tie Up or Position (Head/Bicep, Double Biceps, Double Wrists, Underhook)

(3:82)   **(3:83)**

(3:84)

(3:85)

From a square stance, cheat your foot that is closest to the duck side forward approximately six inches (3:82). Change your level as you step forward and duck under his armpit while stepping behind the opponent (3:83). The top of your head should barely clear the armpit. Dropping to your knee (a common habit) wastes time and significantly decreases your chances of success. Turn your head toward his back (3:84). Using your head, push the opponent forward as you pivot on your trail leg. The torque created by pivoting on the trail leg and pushing with the head is critical to success in Duckunders. Stay close to the opponent's back and chase him if necessary to stay close. Step behind your opponent, lower your level, and lock your hands around his waist with the thumb lock. (3:85)

Farside Duckunder

Tie Up or Position (Double Biceps, Double Wrist, Underhook)

(3:86)

The Farside Duckunder is basically the same as the Basic Duckunder, except rather than stepping around the opponent, you take a quick jab step with your 'cheat foot' (3:86). When he reacts by stepping back, lower your level and take a step with the opposite leg and execute the Duckunder to the far (opposite) side. Lock your hands as in the regular Duckunder.

Duckunder From An Underhook

(3:87)

(3:88)

(3:89)

Although the action on most takedowns is the same regardless of the tieup, Duckunders off the Underhook require adjustments because of your foot and head position.

After securing the Underhook, raise your under hooked elbow until it is parallel to the mat.(3:87) Lower your level and swim your head to his back (3:88) making sure the top of your head grazes his armpit. Create torque by pivoting on the trail leg, pushing with your head (3:89), and rotating your hips as with the Basic Duckunder.

Remember to stay as close as possible to his back to prevent him from creating distance. Chase him (literally) if necessary to stay close. Lock your hands around his waist as in previous Duckunders.

Duckunder To The Mat

(3:90)   **(3:91)**

It is possible to take the opponent directly to the mat with a Regular Duckunder. Rather than release his head after ducking, hold onto it tightly. Drop all your weight onto his neck as you step behind him and drop to your knees in a swinging motion. (3:90) His head and neck should be squeezed between your hand and your shoulder.(3:91) After landing on your knees, drive him over to his back.

The Hi Crotch Series

The Hi Crotch is the third most popular takedown at all levels in terms of attempts. It is a versatile move with two variations (inside or outside step), two finishes and an excellent 'second move' if he sprawls.

Basic Hi Crotch with An Inside or Outside Step

Tie up or Position (Double Biceps, Double Wrists, Head and Biceps, Underhook)

(3:92)   **(3:93)**

(3:94)   **(3:95)**

The Basic Hi Crotch may be executed with the inside or outside step. Each has its own advantages. Using the outside step is quicker, but the inside step is better for deep penetration. First, cheat the outside foot forward. Drop to your back knee (3:92) as you put your inside arm, elbow deep, on or near his spine (3:93). Keep your head on his hip, change your hand to his hip, look up to the back of his far shoulder. (3:94) Jerk his hip forward (as if pulling on a lawnmower cord) and pivot behind him. (3:95). An innovative coaching technique is to tell wrestlers to look for the star (imaginary, of course) on his partner's shoulder.

The inside step to the Hi Crotch is identical to the 'drop step'. After stepping up with your trail foot, the steps are the same as with the Outside Step Hi Crotch.

Hi Crotch to a Change Off

(3:96)   **(3:97)**

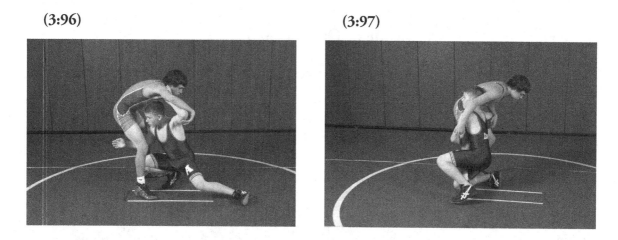

(3:98)   **(3:99)**

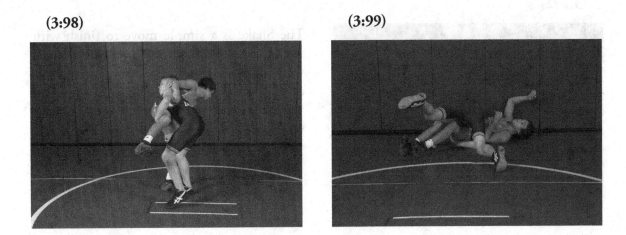

The Change Off is appropriately named because you 'change off' to a Double Leg takedown. It begins the moment after your hand hits the spine. (Placing your hand directly up the spine prevents your opponent from sprawling.(3:96)

The near hand grabs the near knee, as the 'crotch hand' grabs the far knee (3:97). Pushing laterally with your head, and drive off your outside foot, lift (3:98) and dump him to the mat for a takedown (3:99).

Second Moves When Your Opponent Sprawls During Hi Crotch Attempt.

If the opponent sprawls as you attempt a Hi Crotch, keep your head on his outside hip and lock your hands. Three options are available from this position; The Snake, the Wayne Roll, and the Crackdown. First, lock the hands around the single leg and establish a solid base.

Snake

(3:100)   **(3:101)**

(3:102)

The Snake is a simple move to finish with after the sprawl. Simply unlock your hands, wrap (snake) your outside arm around his calf and grab the lower leg (3:100). Sit out on your inside hip as you push backward with your head (3:101). Turn behind him and gain control.(3:102)

Wayne Roll From a Defensive Crossface and Far Ankle

(3:103)

(3:104)

(3:105)

(3:106)

(3:107)

The Wayne Roll is part of the Granby Series and is very effective if your opponent sprawls to prevent a Hi Crotch. With your hands locked tightly (3:103), pull his leg in close to your chest (3:104). Reach back, grab his wrist, pull it off your ankle and place it around your waist (3:105). Slide your outside knee forward (3:106). As your hips fall to the mat, whip your outside elbow out front as a pivot point. It is imperative to post your elbow and hold your head up. With your other arm still holding the knee, throw his leg over, swap-off in mid-air to secure the near (bottom) leg (3:107), and grab a two-on-one on his arm.

Crackdown

(3:108)

(3:109)

The Crackdown begins with the hands locked tightly around his knee. Pull the knee toward your chest as you drive your shoulder into his upper thigh (3:108). Unlock your hands and swim your outside hand up and around the opponent's waist (3:109).

The Fireman's Series

The Basic Fireman's Carry was appropriately name after the position firefighters use to carry victims from a burning structure. Since its inception, the Fireman's Roll, Outside Fireman's Carry, and many 'second moves' following the opponent's sprawl have been developed.

The Basic Fireman's Carry

Tie up or Position (Double Biceps, Head and Biceps, Overhook)

(3:110)

(3:111)

The Basic Fireman's Carry may be executed from one or both knees. The original version was performed from a single knee, but either variety is equally effective.

The move begins as you step in with your lead foot and drop to your back knee (3:110). Pull his arm securely around your neck, and clamp it to your side with pressure from your hand, wrist, and upper arm. Reach directly up his spine, elbow deep. Pull down on arm and lift on his crotch dumping him to his back (3:111). Stay erect until he hits the mat and then immediately cover him.

Fireman's Roll

Tie up or Position (Head and Biceps, Double Biceps, Overhook)

(3:112)

(3:113)

The only difference between the Fireman's Carry and the Fireman's Roll is your foot position. After stepping in with your lead foot (3:112), rather than dropping to your back knee, sit to your opposite hip (3:113), and roll up your side to your shoulder. Finish the move by sitting through and attacking his head.

Outside Fireman's Carry

Tie up or Position (Double Biceps, Head and Biceps, Overhook)

(3:114)

(3:115)

(3:116)

The Outside Fireman's Carry attacks the outside leg and is a low risk move. It is 'low risk' because you are not required to go underneath your opponent and are not in trouble if he sprawls.

The wrapping of your opponent's arm around your neck (3:114) must be timed to coincide with your Dropstep toward his outside leg (3:115). Hold his arm securely by clamping it to your body, hook his knee with your hand and wrist, roll up your side, and throw his leg over forcing him to his back. (3:116) Sit through to your inside hip and attack his head.

Technique if Your Opponent Sprawls During Fireman's

Each of the 'second moves' requires you to square up (parallel to your opponent) and establish a solid base with your knees underneath your chest.

Barrel Roll

(3:117)

(3:118)

(3:119)

The Barrel Roll is named after the lateral rolling of the offensive wrestler to his side. Once you establish your base, pull downward on the trapped elbow until your shoulder touches the mat. As you drop your shoulder to the mat (3:117), throw your outside arm up and over his body, forcing him to his side.(3:118) Finish the move by sitting through to your hip and attacking his head. (3:119)

Knee Tap

(3:120)

(3:121)

(3:122)

After squaring up, raise your upper body to pull your opponent's knees forward and obviously, closer to you. (3:120) Reach across with your free arm (straightened) and block his knee by posting your hand on the mat (3:121). Pull down hard on his elbow to dump him to his side.(3:122). Cover him by sitting through to your inside hip.

Sucker Drag

(3:123)

(3:124)

(3:125)

The Sucker Drag begins by grabbing your opponent's controlled arm with both hands (3:123). Release your grip with the bottom hand and step up with your outside foot (3:124). Turn your upper body laterally as you drag your opponent's arm through. (3:125) Reach over his back to gain control and a takedown.

Frog Hop to a Single Leg Takedown

(3:126)

(3:127)

The Frog Hop to a Single Leg is executed from the same position as the Sucker Drag.
Release your grip with both hands (3:126), and hop like a frog forward grabbing a Single Leg and trapping his arm (3:127). From this position, use technique described in the Single Leg takedown section.

The Snap Drag-Shuck Series

The Snap Drag-Shuck Series has rapidly grown in popularity over the last few years. The series requires minimal energy and is very effective when the opponent is pushing or leaning into you.

The Cross Elbow Shuck

Tie up or Position (Collar Tie)

(3:128)

(3:129)

(3:130) **(3:131)**

The Cross Elbow Shuck is an excellent move to use during a match and also an excellent lead-up move to emphasize proper elbow movement in the Regular Shuck.

With a staggered stance and Collar Tieup, reach across and grab your own biceps (3:128). Make sure you trap your opponent's elbow with your own elbow (3:129). Holding your opponent's head tightly, raise your 'trapping' elbow hard, pushing the opponent's biceps toward his ear (3:130). As you push, be sure to tilt your head to the side, step back slightly with your opposite foot to allow the opponent's hand to come off your neck. Make the move powerful and quick. Lock your hands in a headlock position (3:131) capturing his arm and head or around his waist.

Regular Elbow Shuck

Tie up or Position (Collar Tieup)

(3:132) **(3:133)**

(3:134)

The Regular Elbow Shuck is almost identical to the Cross Elbow Shuck, with one exception. Rather than reaching across to the far biceps, place your forearm slightly above the opponent's elbow (3:132), torque your upper body thrusting him forward (3:133, 3:134) and follow through as in the Cross Elbow Shuck.

Shuck to a Garner Roll

(3:135)

(3:136)

(3:137)

After securing the headlock from behind your opponent, step forward with your outside leg (3:135) and hook his outside leg with the toe of your inside leg. Continue to squeeze tightly on the headlock, drop to your outside knee (3:136), jerk hard on his upperbody, and roll through using the toe hook to lift your opponent.(3:137) Squeeze hard and maintain the leg lift.

If your opponent manages to free his leg, turn your stomach toward the mat or allow him to turn to his stomach.

Shuck on the Mat

Tie up or Position (Collar Tieup)

(3:138)

(3:139)

(3:140)

A versatile move, the Regular Elbow Shuck is very effective 'down on the mat'(3:138). On both knees and in a Collar Tieup, step up with your outside foot (3:139), and Elbow Shuck your opponent to the mat (3:140).

Double Arm Shuck

Tie up or Position (Collar Tieup)

(3:141)

(3:142)

The Double Arm Shuck is a unique move that is not widely used, or even known. From the Collar Tieup, reach across and grab the opponent's biceps-triceps from underneath. Simultaneously turn your shoulder inward, trapping both elbows and essentially, both his arms (3:141). Torque your hips and throw his arms forward with a 'shucking' motion. During the shuck, reach around the opponent's waist with the opposite hand (3:142) and follow through by locking your hands around his waist

The Throwby

Tie up or Position (Collar Tieup)

(3:143)

(3:144)

The Throwby is primarily a move for the heavier weight classes and is executed from a basic Collar Tieup and square stance. Take your hand from the elbow, reach under the opponent's arm and place it flat on his upper back. (3:143). Lower your level by bending your legs, pop your elbow up and forward quickly as you turn your head laterally and step behind him (3:144).

Throwby from Double Underhooks

Tie up or Position (Double Underhook)

(3:145)

(3:146)

From a staggered stance and Double Underhook position (3:145), raise both your elbows until they are parallel to the mat. Pull downward on your opponent's far shoulder and throw your near elbow up and forward as you step behind him. Follow through by locking your hands around his waist. (3:146)

The Snap Drag

Tie up or Position (Collar Tieup)

(3:147)

(3:148)

(3:149)   **(3:150)**

The Snap Drag (sometimes referred to as the Passby) begins as you reach over the opponent's near arm and post his chest with a closed fist and straight arm (3:147). Using your arm only, push into him to encourage him to react and push back. Rotate your palm upward, reach inside his upper arm grabbing it securely (3:148). As you turn your head laterally, jerk the upper arm forward (3:149), and step behind him with the outside foot. (3:150)

Follow through by securing a waist lock.

The Snap / Snap Down Series

The Snap/Snap Down series is a versatile series of moves requiring minimal effort. Several of the 'second moves' can be done from the standing position or down on the mat.

Basic Snap to a Go Behind

Tie up or Position (Head and Biceps, Double Biceps)

(3:151)   **(3:152)**

(3:153)   **(3:154)**

The Basic Snap works best from the Double Biceps (3:151), although it can be effective from the Head and Biceps Tieup. The advantage of the Double Biceps is that momentum and power are created when the hand is moved from one biceps to cup the neck and snap the head downward. After moving the hand to the neck, snap the head downward toward your lead foot (3:152). As the opponent goes down, move your lead foot backwards and sprawl on top of him or block his arm with the back of your opposite hand (3:153) and spin around behind him to secure a takedown (3:154).

Snap To Wrist Trap

(3:155)   **(3:156)**

(3:157)

(3:158)

(3:159)

(3:160)

After snapping the opponent to the mat, under hook the arm opposite the snap hand (3:155), and hook his head with your snapping arm. Reach across and grab his wrist on the under hooked side (3:156). Raise your hips very high and put your head behind his near armpit (3:157). With powerful torque, jerk up on the wrist and roll through (3:158). Post your hand that is under hooked on the mat (3:159). Squeeze his head tightly and secure a pin (3:160).

Snap to a Standing Wrist Trap

(3:161)

(3:162)

(3:163)

(3:164)

(3:165)

The Snap to a Standing Wrist Trap is a relatively new move and, can work even against superior opponents. The Snap is only hard enough to get the opponent's head down to your waist level. As you snap, under hook his arm with your other hand and allow the snapping hand to hook his head quickly. Reach toward the underhooked side and grab the opponent's wrist in the standard 'Wrist Trap' position. (3:161) Step toward the trapped wrist side to make him step forward creating an angle. (3:162) Place your head behind his arm pit and pull his wrist up hard. (3:163). Torque your hips taking him directly to his back (3:164) Roll through, post your hand on the mat and pin him (3:165).

Snap to Wrist Trap Go Behind

(3:166)   **(3:167)**

(3:168)   **(3:169)**

The Wrist Trap move is basically a 'once per match' move. However, there is an alterative move that works from the exact same position called the 'Go Behind'. From the 'Wrist Trap' position on the mat, raise your hips while holding the wrist up tightly (3:166). Pull your under hook arm out (3:167), pull his wrist up, and spin around behind the opponent for control (3:168, 3:169) This is an excellent move for the heavier weights who usually don't like rolling across their backs.

Snap to Whipover

(3:170) **(3:171)**

(3:172) **(3:173)**

From the Snap Down to under hook and head hook position (3:170), step up with your outside foot for power (3:171). Pushing off your posted foot, whip your opponent to his back (3:172). Post your hand on the mat, spread your legs to establish a solid base, hold your head up, and also raise his head off the mat (3:173) to prevent a bridge.

Front Headlock Series

The Front Headlock Series has grown tremendously in popularity during recent years. Several secondary moves from the front headlock position make it a valuable weapon in an arsenal of technique. Overall, the Front Headlock Series is very similar to the Snapdown series. The primary differences between the two are hand and head position after the snap.

Front Headlock, Go Behind

Tie up or Position (Head and Biceps, Double Biceps)

(3:174)   **(3:175)**

(3:176)   **(3:177)**

Use the same action as in the Snapdown series to get your opponent to his knees. Lock your hands behind his triceps while keeping your elbow high. Place your head directly behind the triceps area (in the hole) (3:174). Make sure your hips are high, your knees are off the mat and you are driving your shoulder into the back of his neck to create pressure.(3:175) Reach around his far waist with the near hand (3:176) and go behind for a takedown (3:177).

Front Headlock to Cradle

(3:178)

(3:179)

(3:180)

(3:181)

(3:182)

From the Front Headlock position, with the 'head in the hole' (3:178), maintaining pressure (3:179)reach around and grab the opponent's knee pulling it toward his head (3:180). Lock your hands, placing him in a cradle (3:181) and turn him to his back. (3:182).

Front Headlock to Shuck

(3:183)

(3:184)

(3:185)

From the Front Headlock position, reach around to grab the knee as if to hook up a cradle. When the opponent circles his legs away to avoid the cradle, chase him by running around on the balls of your feet. (3:183). As you are 'chasing him', stop, and whip him hard in the direction of his momentum with the arm around the his head (3:184). Follow through and securing control by grabbing his arm and waist, or an ankle. (3:185)

Front Headlock to Knee Pull

(3:186)

From the Front Headlock position, relax the pressure pushing down on your opponent's neck. Pull up slightly encouraging him to step up with his outside foot. Dip your inside shoulder, release your locked hands grip, and reach to grab his raised knee (3:186). Drive your opponent to his back, securing a takedown.

Standing Front Headlock to Heel Pick

As with the Snap to Wrist Trap, the Snap to the Front Headlock is practical from the standing position. Once you have the Front Headlock secured with your head 'in the hole', step to the side your head is on making the opponent step also. Torque your opponent's upper body hard as you drop to your inside knee and grab his ankle. Hold on to the Headlock, reach over his ankle and lock your hands in the cradle position.

Standing Front Headlock to Cradle

(3:187)

(3:188)

(3:189)

From the Standing Front Headlock position, pressure down (3:187), step around, reach around the near knee, lock your hands and assume the cradle position (3:188). Pull your opponent to the mat for a takedown. (3:189)

Standing Front Headlock to Flying Cradle

(3:190)

(3:191)

(3:192)

From the Front Headlock position, release your grip, take the hand around the near arm and grab his wrist. Raise your arm pulling his arm upward, step forward and duck under the arm (3:190).Sit to your inside hip as you reach around the knee (3:191) and lock your hands in a cradle (3:192).

Heel Pick Series

The Heel Pick, often referred to as the Ankle Pick, Series requires repeated drill and special focus on setups. Heel picks are effective standing and, in specific situations, down on the mat. As a coaching point, referring to the series as 'Heel Pick' rather than 'Ankle Pick', makes the wrestler focus his attention on grabbing lower on the leg, and creating better leverage.

Far Heel Pick

Tie up or Position (Head and Biceps)

(3:193)

(3:194)

(3:195)

The basic move in the Heel Pick Series is the Far Heel Pick. From the Head and Biceps Tieup, step, and circle away from the heel to be attacked. Pull down and around on the head and the biceps. (3:193). As your opponent's foot hits the mat, pull down hard on his head and point your elbow toward his foot. Make sure his head is below your chest. Drop to your outside knee, reach for and grab the heel (3:194). Hold the heel, and in an arms-crossing motion, throw him to his back (3:195). Cover him for control and a takedown.

Initially (while drilling), requiring the attacking wrestler to 'chop the mat' three times behind the opponent's heel before following through, focuses his attention on grabbing the heel rather than the lower leg or calf

Near Heel Pick

Tie up or Position (Head and Biceps, Collar Tie)

(3:196)

(3:197)

(3:198)

The Near Heel Pick can be executed from two tieups. The reason is that securing the opponent's head to your shoulder is an important key to the move. Cupping his head tightly, circle away from the near heel. As he plants his foot, quickly change direction and pull downward on the head as you drop to your inside knee (3:196). While squeezing his head against your shoulder, reach across and grab the near heel. (3:197) Pull downward on the head and up on the heel to take him to his back (3:198). Hold the head tightly and keep the leg up high to secure a nearfall.

Forearm Shuck

Tie up or Position (Head and Biceps)

(3:199)

(3:200)

(3:201)

The Forearm Shuck is done only from the Head and Biceps Tieup as your head must be free (3:199). When attempting a Far Heel Pick, the opponent will sometimes anticipate the move and step back with the foot to be attacked and drop to his knees. Step up with your outside foot (3:200) and with the opponent's head cupped hard, snap your forearm hard across your body to shuck him to the mat (3:201). The tendency to 'extend your arm and push him away' must be controlled by keeping your elbow locked at 90 degrees as you shuck him around.

Upper Body Moves

Upper body moves add a new dimension to your wrestling ability. Many opponents are uncomfortable in 'over and under' and 'over hook and under hook' situations. They are very vulnerable to throws, hugs, snags, blocks, locks, trips and tosses from these tieups.

Pummeling

(3:202)

Pummeling, often referred to in certain geographic areas as 'swimming', is a sound developmental drill for securing the appropriate tieup for the upper body technique. Starting with both wrestlers in the 'over and under' position, each attempts to 'swim' his overhooking hand to the inside to gain an advantage. (3:202). Once inside, grab the opponent's lat firmly to secure the 'Double Underhook' position. It is often necessary to turn your upper body sideways to enable your arm to get through. Both wrestlers are working for inside position. Pummeling or 'swimming' is an excellent conditioning drill, especially for the heavier weights that are in the situation more frequently.

Bear Hug

Tie up or Position (Head and Biceps, Double Biceps, Over and Under)

(3:203)

(3:204)

(3:205)

The most basic move from the 'over and under' position is the Bear Hug. Swim the over hooking arm (from the staggered stance), step forward with your lead foot and lower your level, lock your hands in the opponent's lower back (3:203). Step inside, hook the leg opposite your head for balance (3:204), and throw him to his back. (3:205). Keeping your hands locked is legal as you took him directly from his feet to his back in a pinning combination.

Driving your shoulder into his body and raising your hips will help secure the fall. From the other tieups listed, simply release your grip, step in, lock your hands, and follow through.

Body Lock

Tie up or Position (Head and Biceps, Double Biceps, Over and Under)

(3:206)

(3:207)

(3:208)

The second most popular move from the 'over and under' position is the Body Lock. From the staggered stance, step forward with your lead foot, lower your level, lock your hands in the opponent's lower back trapping the arm (3:206). Step beside his outside foot with your trail leg (3:207) to block his knee. Throw him laterally over your knee to his back. (3:208). Keeping your hands locked is legal as you took him directly from his feet to his back in a pinning combination. From the other tieups listed, quickly release your grip, step in, lock your hands in his lower back trapping the arm, and follow through tossing him to his back.

Hip Toss Variations

Tie up or Position (Overhook, Underhook, Over and Under)

The major difference in the variations is the footwork involved. All involve stepping into and across the opponent, placing your hips under his, pulling downward on his upper body and popping your hips up tossing him to his back.

Dariel W. Daniel

From The Overhook

(3:209) **(3:210)**

(3:211) **(3:212)**

From the Overhook Tie, slide your other hand downward to the opponent's biceps and grab it tightly (3:209). Step across his body as you bend your legs slightly and pull downward on his arms and pop your hips up hard lifting him off the mat (3:210) As you continue to pull downward on his upper body toss him to his back (3:211, 3:212).

Far Knee Pick

Tie up or Position (Underhook)

The Far Knee Pick is worked from the standard Underhook position. Stepping directly toward your opponent's far foot with your lead foot, grab the far knee with your other hand and, drive through your opponent taking him to the mat.

Knee Snag

Tie up or Position (Over and Under)

(3:213)

(3:214)

(3:215)

(3:216)

(3:217)

From a square stance and an 'Over and Under' tie, step laterally with your foot opposite the Overhook (3:213). Pull downward on his arm as you step back and around with your other foot. (3:214) Reach across with your other hand and snag his knee (with your hand cupped). (3:215). Pull his knee inward as you drive your shoulder down into his shoulder forcing him to the mat. (3:216). Place your arm around his waist to secure control. (3:217). The Knee Snag is a technique that requires precise timing. As he is moving forward and his foot plants on the mat, snag the knee (cup the outside ligaments with your fingers) and drive your shoulder into his shoulder immediately. Allow your opponent to land on the mat first and then cover him.

Thigh Block

Tie up or Position (Over and Under)

(3:218)

(3:219)

From a square stance and 'Over and Under' tie, pull down hard on his shoulder and arm making him bend his knees. Step back with your foot that is opposite the over hook as you reach across with your over hooked hand and grab the top of his thigh (3:218). Make sure your arm is rotated and your elbow is locked. Turn your shoulder downward and pry upward on his ribcage (3:219) throwing him to the mat. Place your arm around his waist to secure control. Always allow the opponent to land on the mat first and then cover him.

Inside Trip

Tie up or Position (Over and Under)

(3:220)

(3:221)

From the 'Over and Under' tieup, pull downward hard on your opponent's arm and shoulder to make him bend his knees. Step between your opponent's legs and hook his leg opposite your head (3:220). Drive forward hard and drop to your knees, tripping him to his back (3:221).

CHAPTER 4

Breakdowns: Destroying His Base

Breakdowns, as the name implies, are designed to 'break' the opponent off his base and place him in a more vulnerable position for tilts, turns, and pinning combinations. Although some pinning moves are designed to be executed directly from the 'referee's position', most require preliminary action to destroy his 'base' position.

Top Positions—Depending on the technique one intends to execute, there are four possible variations in the top position, with each having its own advantages and disadvantages.

(4:1)   **(4:2)**

(4:4)

(4:3)

(4:5)

Inside Knee Up (4:1)
Outside Knee Up (4:2)
Both Knees Down (4:3)
Optional Start (4:4, 4:5)

Cheating Is Okay!

Cheating, in a wrestling sense, is perfectly legal and even recommended to gain an advantage in position to execute a move. Though the rule book specifies a standard starting position, certain variances are allowed and should be used to one's advantage.

'Cheating' forward, to his hips, toward his feet, or to a perpendicular position can increase the success rate of executing certain techniques. Every advantage, however small, may ultimately be the deciding factor in victory. Though football has always been considered a 'game of inches', wrestling is the 'sport of inches'.

Basic Breakdowns

Arm Chop-Knee Drive

(4:6)

(4:7)

The Arm Chop along with the Knee Drive is probably the most widely used breakdown at every level of competition. The offensive wrestler rotates his wrist to chop the opponent's elbow (4:6) as he simultaneously grabs a tight waist. Pushing forward off his back foot, he drives his knee forward into the bottom man's hips to 'flatten him out'. (4:7)

Far Knee-Far Ankle

(4:8)

Cheating to a perpendicular position close to the opponent's hips allows for better and quicker grabbing of the far knee and far ankle. On the whistle, grab the opponent's far knee with your outside hand (on the elbow). Grab his far ankle with your arm that is around his waist. (4:8) Make sure that your hands are cupped (no thumbs) as you pull his legs underneath you to complete the breakdown.

Far Waist-Far Ankle

(4:9)

Cheating back toward the opponent's hips allows for better and quicker grabbing of the far waist and far ankle. On the whistle, move the hand on the elbow to the far waist position as you simultaneously grab the far ankle with a cupped hand. (4:9) Though it is commonly called the ankle, the shoelaces are actually grabbed for better leverage and power. Pushing off your back foot, drive his leg forward to break him down.

Dariel W. Daniel

Near Waist-Near Ankle

(4:10) **(4:11)**

(4:12) **(4:13)**

Cheating back toward the opponent's hips allows for better and quicker grabbing of the near ankle. Your inside arm remains around your opponent's waist. In a pivoting action of the knees, your back knee goes down as your front knee rotates upward. (4:10) Grab the shoelaces of the near foot and jerk it back over your thigh. (4:11) Keeping your head in front of his hips, grab behind his far thigh with your front hand (formerly on the laces) (4:12) and drop into a Navy Ride position. (4:13)

Crossface-Far Ankle

(4:14)

(4:15)

Cheating to a more perpendicular position than normal allows for a better and quicker Crossface and Far Ankle. On the whistle, crossface the opponent and grab his far arm with your cupped hand above his elbow. (4:14) Release his waist and, using a cupped hand, grab his far ankle. Jerk both (arm and ankle) toward your body as you pull him underneath you and complete the breakdown. (4:15)

Head Lever-Tight Waist

(4:16)

(4:17)

The Head Lever and Tight Waist seems to have lost much of the popularity it had in the 60's and 70's, but is still a sound breakdown with great versatility for follow-up moves. From the standard starting position, drop your hand from his elbow to his near wrist and squeeze it tightly. As you are dropping your hand, move the top of your head to his armpit and secure a tight waist simultaneously. (4:16) Using your head as a fulcrum, pull his arm back to lock it out and using the tight waist, pull him down to his side (4:17). Maintain pressure by forcing your head into the back of his armpit and elevating your hips. Keep a very tight grip around his waist to secure control and a very solid breakdown.

Knee Drop-Far Ankle

(4:18)

(4:19)

Considered unethical by some coaches, the painful Knee Drop-Far Ankle is extremely effective. From a standard starting position, with the back knee up, lower the knee until it is slightly above the opponent's ankle.(4:18) Depending on the official's position, your knee might even touch the ankle slightly. On the whistle, drop your knee hard on the opponent's ankle stopping his first move. (4:19). Simultaneously, grab his far knee and far ankle, and drive hard forcing your opponent to his side completely broken down.

Jump Sides

(4:20)

(4:21)

Appropriately named, Jump Sides means that, on the whistle, you must jump from one side (4:20) of the opponent to the other. and 'spring' across the opponent hitting him in the stomach with a clenched fist and chopping his elbow at the same time. (4:21) The momentum created by the explosive 'jump' is very effective in not only stopping the opponent's first move, but also breaking him down to his stomach.

Leg Control Techniques after the Breakdown

Controlling the opponent's legs after a breakdown can serve multiple purposes and each provides you an advantage. First, it restricts the opponent's motion and limits his options regarding technique. As he struggles to free his legs, an offensive move is secondary in his mind. Secondly, since his motion is restricted, it provides and excellent opportunity to set up a pinning combination. Third, in certain situations, total leg control may be purposely used to 'kill some clock' (allow time to pass) in a close match or where fatigue is becoming an issue. Only use the rides until the official instructs you to "let the legs go". Even after the verbal caution, you may choose to continue to maintain the position until the referee stops the match and gives an official warning.

Knee In-Toe Out (near leg)

(4:22)

With your weight pressing on his near hip, place your knee inside his knee. With your toe, force his lower leg inward creating pressure on the knee joint as you pressure outward with your knee. (4:22)

Knees Out-Toes In

(4:23)

With your hips covering his hips, place your knees outside both his knees. With your toes, force his lower legs outward creating pressure on the knee joints as you pressure inward with your knees. (4:23)

Lace

(4:24)

With your hips covering his hips, use your toe to raise his lower leg (far leg). Hook his near leg with your toe, trapping the far leg. (4:24) Now, your opponent must focus on freeing his leg before he can establish a solid base from which to move. With practice, this maneuver is easily executed without looking back toward the feet.

Figure 4 Thigh

(4:25)

(4:26)

With your hips covering his hips, use your toe to raise his lower leg (near leg). Without looking, reach back and grab the laces of his near shoe with your cupped hand. Holding the laces, push off the outside foot and lunge forward raising his thigh off the mat. (4:25)

Slide your lower leg (inside leg) under his thigh and then hook it to create a Figure 4. (4:26) The Figure 4 on the Thigh technique is very effective and has several 'second moves' that take him toward his back.

CHAPTER 5

Ride, Baby, Ride!

In the wrestling arena, riding refers to the act of controlling the opponent for a period of time until a potential scoring or pinning situation is achieved. Many wrestlers are able to ride the opponent aggressively and actually 'wear the opponent down' by forcing him to constantly defend offensive moves and also carry his (offensive wrestler) weight. Obviously, riding requires controlling one or more body parts (hips, arms, ankles, wrists) of the opponent.

Basic Rides

Cross Wrist Ride

(5:1)

After chopping the opponent's near elbow, guide his lower arm across his body and secure his wrist. (5:1) Hold the wrist tightly against his hip and look for options including hooks and the Turkey Bar.

Turkey Bar Ride

(5:2)

The Turkey Bar is an option from the Cross Wrist Ride. Using your near arm, slide your forearm between your opponent's ribs and his biceps to secure a Chickenwing.

(5:2) Keep your biceps above his elbow to keep it legal. A Chickenwing with your opponent on his knees with his wrist trapped is a Turkey Bar Ride. Stacks, tilts, and pins are secondary moves from this position.

Spiral Ride

(5:3)   **(5:4)**

The Spiral Ride was appropriately name because of the rotating or 'spiraling' action created by its application. From the referee's position, grab his near or far shoulder with your outside hand. The hand around his waist moves immediately to the inside of his far thigh with your palm pointed outwards. (5:3) Straighten your outside arm, pry on the thigh, hold his shoulder tightly, and drive around (use your legs) clockwise (5:4). As with other rides, several options for pins and tilts are immediately available.

Crossbody Ride

(5:5)

I often refer to the Crossbody Ride as the 'Great Equalizer'. Competency with the Crossbody Ride levels the 'playing field' for wrestlers who are facing stronger or more experienced opponents. Although it takes time to develop confidence and competency, it takes even more time to learn to defend or escape this very unique ride. The Guillotine, Banana Split, Reverse Double Crossface, Far Side Power Half, and other options are available once the Crossbody Ride is applied.

(5:6) **(5:7)**

(5:8) **(5:9)**

There are three basic ways to apply the Crossbody Ride, including the Arm Chop-Hip Slide, Bump to Elbow Block, and the Spiral.

1. Arm Chop-HipSlide

   As you chop his near arm, pull your opponent to his side with a tight waist. (5:5) Slide on your outside hip as you bump his inside knee with yours. As he begins to return to his base, slide your outside leg into the Crossbody Ride position (5:6). The most important thing to remember regarding a Crossbody Ride is to keep your hips on top of his hips!

2. Bump to Elbow Block

   With your upper body, bump your opponent forward to stop his first move. With your outside forearm, block his elbow to prevent him from reaching back. Slide your leg in, securing the Crossbody Ride position (5:7). Make sure your hips stay on TOP of your opponent's hips.

3. Spiral

   Probably the most difficult of the options allowing you to apply a Crossbody is the Spiral. As you drive around (clockwise), your opponent's outside knee will raise off the mat. (5:8) Jump across and put your leg in (5:9) to secure the Crossbody Ride.

Double Grapevine

(5:10)

(5:11)

The Double Grapevine requires only one additional step to those described in the Crossbody Ride. After one leg has been inserted, simply put the other leg in as well for the Double Grapevine (5:10). The Double Grapevine earned its name by the vine-like wrapping of your legs around both of your opponent's legs. If the opponent remains on his base, arch and drive forward with both your forearms on his lower arms to break him down to his stomach. (5:11)

Garner Ride

(5:12)

(5:13)

Although it can potentially be used to secure a nearfall or pin, we used the Garner Ride primarily to 'kill a few seconds of time'. Bump the opponent (5:12) and immediately lock your hands in a nearside headlock (5:13), squeezing as hard as possible. Due to the pressure on his neck, it will be almost impossible to escape. Most opponents try to hook your inside leg (especially if you are yelling "Don't let him hook your leg"). If he decides to hook your leg (most do), the Garner Roll in either direction becomes an option.

Turk

The Turk (I'm guessing it originated in Turkey) can be applied from several positions and is a very difficult ride from which to escape.

Skilled wrestlers who are competent with the Turk usually earn nearfall points and frequently a pin with the addition of arm hooks. The two most common ways to get into a Turk position consist of one on the mat and one standing.

On The Mat

(5:14)

(5:15)

(5:16)

With your outside arm, grab your opponent's far waist. Hook his near thigh with your inside arm. (5:14) Lift his thigh and step over his far leg. (5:15) Drop step forward, arch your back, raise your leg (lifting his leg), post both hands, and keep your head up. (5:16)

Standing

(5:17)

(5:18)

(5:19)

After picking up a single, allow your opponent's upper body to drop.(5:17) Keeping the near thigh secured, step over his far leg, (5:18) drop step forward, arch your back and raise your leg, post both hands, and keep your head up. Using the inside arm to wrap the opponent's head and pull it laterally usually results in a nearfall or pin. (5:19)

Navy Ride

(5:20)

(5:21)

The Navy ride was very popular in the late 60's and early 70's. Though it has seemingly lost some of its popularity, it is still an effective technique.

With your outside knee down in the starting position, pivot to your inside knee. As you pivot, release your grip on your opponent's elbow and grab the instep (laces) of his near foot. Using the momentum created by the pivot, jerk the ankle straight back over your thigh. (5:20) Release your grip on his ankle and, lowering your level, scoop the back of his far thigh.(5:21) As he falls to the mat, keep your head in front and secure a tight grip on his waist with your outside arm. (5:22) There are also several pin, or nearfall options from the Navy Ride.

CHAPTER 6

Tilts and Pinning Combinations

Considered the ultimate in wrestling by many, a pin excites the crowd, 'fires up' the team, and earns maximum points in dual or tournament competition. T-shirts nationwide exclaim "Pinning Is Everything". Even with the onset of the modern team scoring system, pins are still the ultimate and decisive action, but technical falls and major decisions are not far behind. Tech falls and major decisions often demonstrate more skill superiority than a quick pin.

Currently, a technical fall is earned when one competitor earns a fifteen point lead in match scoring. A major decision is earned when a competitor has an eight to fourteen point lead at the match's conclusion.

A tilt is defined as placing one's opponent in a position where his upper body (scapula area) is held at an angle of forty-five degrees or less (in reference to the mat) for two or more seconds. Near fall points are earned from this position. If the opponent bridges during the tilt, but of his scapula areas are held within four inches of the mat for two or more consecutive seconds, near fall points are earned.

Half Nelson Series

After watching thousands of matches at all levels, I determined the half nelson series to be the most widely used pinning technique, with the greatest success rate, of any in the nation.

Several variations of the half nelson exist and all are very effective at every level.

Regular Half

(6:1) **(6:2)**

(6:3) **(6:4)**

The Regular or Basic Half should be the first pinning technique taught to beginning wrestlers. Though it is very basic, it is probably the most improperly taught and incorrectly applied technique in wrestling.

When applying a Basic Half, your hand goes under your opponent's near shoulder and your hand is placed on the back of his head. The old-fashioned way of applying it was to put your hand on his neck and turn him over to his back by driving perpendicularly . . . . not any more!

Research has shown placing your hand on the back of his head (6:1), driving forward with your legs, and raising your elbow (6:2) creates more force and much better leverage. Once his elbow is raised, scoop his head with your cupped hand, place your arm around his neck, lower your armpit to his neck, drop your chest rather than check, and secure the deep half before slowly turning your opponent to his back.(6:3) Once your opponent is on his back, squeeze his neck tightly, raise your elbow (preventing a bridge), post your opposite hand, spread your feet and get on your toes transferring your weight to his chest.(6:4)It is also helpful to grab your own shoulder to prevent your opponent from getting his arm through and turning to his stomach.

Note: Always secure the deep half before turning your opponent past ninety degrees. It is much easier to get it tight in the beginning rather than attempt to 'sink it' as he scrambles to prevent a pin.

Power Half

(6:5)

(6:6)

(6:7)

(6:8)

(6:9)

The Power Half is very similar to the Regular Half nelson, with the exception of assistance from your other hand. The Power Half begins are your place your wrist at the base of your opponent's skull with your palm up. Pressing downward hard, reach underneath his near shoulder and lock your hands (6:5). Press your shoulder toward your wrist squeezing his shoulder (6:6). As you continue to press on his neck and squeeze his shoulder, get on your toes and drive forward hard (6:7) as your raise your (and his) elbow (6:6, 6:7). Straighten your arm (6:8) and continue as with the Regular Half. (6:8) As shown in the Regular Half, grasp other shoulder for security if desired.

Re-Half

(6:10)

The Re-Half becomes applicable when the opponent reaches up and grabs your hand to counter your half. With your opposite hand, grab his wrist (6:10), pull it back hard, and continue the regular half. Continue to hold his wrist even after he is on his back.

Trap Half

(6:11)

(6:12)

(6:13)

The Trap Half is basically the same as the re-half with one change. Rather than keeping your hand on your opponent's neck, grab his captured (trapped) wrist with it (6:11) creating a two-on-one situation. (6:12) Drive forward and continue as in the Regular Half.(6:13)

Cross Wrist Series

Cross Wrist Load up Tilt

(6:14)

(6:15)

With the Cross Wrist ride secured, grab the near elbow, place your instep (near) under your opponent's ankle, scoop him into your lap, lift his ankle, and squeeze tightly (6:14). Elevating his foot makes it difficult for him to turn.(6:15)

Cross Wrist, Crossface

(6:16)

(6:17)

(6:18)

With the Cross Wrist secured, use your free hand to secure a Crossface (above the elbow) (6:16). With both arms tied up, step up with your inside foot, jerk your opponent around in a counter-clockwise direction (6:17) whipping him to his back. Lay on top of both his arms to secure a pin.(6:18)

Cross Wrist Head-Stuff

(6:19)

(6:20)

Usually performed somewhat late in a match, the Head-Stuff usually ends in a pin. With the wrist secure trapped, use your forearm of your free arm to quickly stuff the opponent's head underneath his body (6:19). As you press down hard on his knee, push him forward with your hip rolling him onto his shoulders (6:20). A pin is usually imminent.

Heard Roll

(6:21)

(6:22)

(6:23)

(6:24)

The Heard Roll is named for one of my former 3X State Champions, Charlie Heard. With the Cross Wrist secure (6:21), raise your hips high into the air (6:22). With a quick motion, dive underneath your opponent. (6:23) As you grab behind his far thigh, jerk hard on his trapped wrist. Hold his far thigh and wrist tightly, as you stop him on his back (6:24). Rarely does a pin ensue, but nearfalls are practically guaranteed.

Clemson Roll Series

The Clemson Roll series is one of the more versatile series in amateur wrestling. With a minimum of five secondary moves possible, it is a series you want in your 'arsenal of weapons'.

Basic Clemson Roll

(6:25)

(6:26)

With cross wrist control, hook the near elbow tightly (with a cupped hand). Drop your chest behind his near hip and pull back hard on his elbow and wrist. Release your grip on his elbow, reach through his crotch and re-secure your grip on the elbow. Block his inside knee with your inside knee. Jerk on his wrist hard as you duck your head underneath ("Look for cotton in his bellybutton" is a great reminder for ducking the head underneath.) and roll through (6:25). As you begin to roll, focus on stopping him from rolling completely by raising your leg and placing your foot behind his knee (6:26).

Kidney Crusher

(6:27)

(6:28)

After securing a near fall with the basic roll, allow your hand on his elbow to slide to his wrist as he turns to his stomach (6:27). Once he is flat, take your free hand, hook his elbow, place your elbow in his kidney area, lean back forcing him to his back, and lift the far leg. (6:28) as previously.

Half

(6:29)

(6:30)

After earning near fall points from the Kidney Crusher, allow your opponent to build up to his knees by pushing off his free hand. As he reaches his base, reach under his arm and run a Half Nelson making sure to 'sink it' deep before turning him to his back. (6:29, 6:30) Continue to hold his wrist as you work for the pin.

Far Shoulder

(6:31)

Another option, as your opponent builds up to his base, is to grab his far shoulder. Reach underneath his body and cup the far shoulder near his neck. Jerking up on his wrist and jerking down and around on his shoulder forces him to his back (6:31).

Texas Cable

(6:32)

(6:33)

The Texas Cable is a recent addition to the Clemson series. With his wrist still secured in his crotch, reach over your opponent's back, hook his elbow with your elbow, and grab his thigh firmly (6:32). Dive over his body toward his head rolling him to his back (6:33). Hold his far foot up as previously done in the Clemson series.

2 On 1 Series

(6:34)

Appropriately named, the 2 on 1 begins as you control his wrist (lower arm) with your two hands on his near forearm. One hand is on each side of the opponent's body. (6:34)

2 On 1 Tilt

(6:35)

(6:36)

(6:37)

Control his wrist (lower arm) with your two hands on his near forearm. Post your inside foot under his near ankle (6:35). Pull his arm tightly as you roll to your side (6:36), scoop him into your lap, and lift his ankle turning him to his back (6:37).

2 On 1 with Half Nelson

(6:38)

(6:39)

(6:40)

Control his wrist (lower arm) with your two hands on his far forearm. Raise your upper body, straighten your arms, and roll your knuckles underneath (6:38). Rotate your outside elbow forward and get on your toes to transfer your weight (and a lot of pressure) to your opponent's triceps. Release your grip with your near arm, run a half (6:39, 6:40), sink it deep, and drive him to his back.

2 On 1 to Double-Double

(6:41)

The Double-Double varies only slightly from the two-on-one with a half. It is, however, much tighter and more likely to secure a pin. Once the half has been sunk deep around his neck, grab his trapped wrist with the half hand securing a two-on-one situation (6:41). Squeeze hard, hold your head up, and expect a pin. Because both your arms are around both his upper arms, the technique is appropriately called a Double-Double.

Chickenwing Series

(6:42)

The Chickenwing obviously got its name from the position of the defensive man's arm after it is hooked and pulled back. One of the older series in wrestling, the Chickenwing techniques are very difficult to counter.

From the starting position or after a breakdown, hook the defensive man's elbow with your forearm (6:42). It is imperative that your biceps be above his elbow as well as your forearm which is underneath his biceps. Pressure upward with your forearm and downward with your triceps creates tremendous pressure and makes lower arm circulation difficult for him.

Chickenwing with a Half Nelson

(6:43)   **(6:44)**

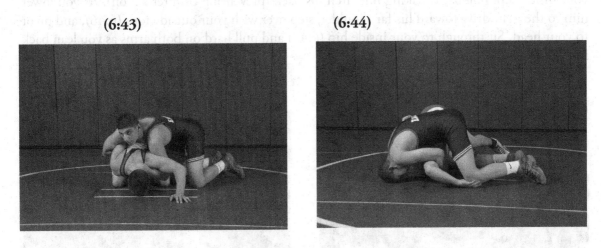

After securing a Chickenwing on the far side, run a deep half to turn him onto his shoulders (6:43) Stay on your knees and post your head for stability (6:44)

Chickenwing with an Arm Hook

(6:45)   **(6:46)**

(6:47)   **(6:48)**

After securing a nearside Chickenwing, under hook your opponent's far elbow (6:45). Sitout to your inside hip, pull back making him arch his back (preventing counter action). As you lower him to the mat, drive toward his far shoulder, step over with your outside foot (6:46), and pivot to your head. Sit through to your inside hip (6:47) and pull hard on both arms as you lean back into his hips (6:48).

Chickenwing With Bar

(6:49)

(6:50)

With the near Chickenwing and Far Bar secured, roll the bar underneath and pressure the triceps by getting on your toes.(6:49) Making sure your biceps remains above his elbow, rotate your hips, grab his shoulder blade (6:50), and slowly drive his scapula toward the mat. Your forearm should be pressuring outward and your triceps pressing downward.

Chickenwing with Arm Hook to Hip Heist

(6:51)

(6:52)

(6:53) (6:54)

After securing a nearside Chickenwing, under hook your opponent's far elbow. Sit out to your inside hip, pull back to make him arch his back (preventing counter action) (6:51). Lowering him to the mat, drive down toward his far shoulder. When the opponent resists by pressuring back, scissor your legs, jerk hard on his arms and turn toward your stomach (6:52, 6:53, 6:54). Sit through as previously described. The same action can be performed with a Double Chickenwing.

Chickenwing with Far Half Nelson

(6:55) (6:56)

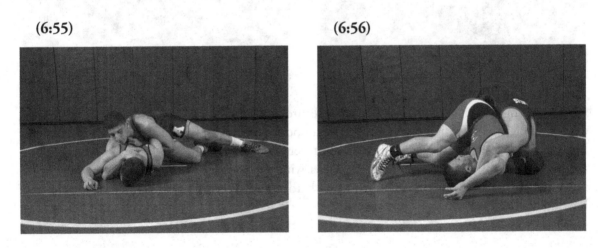

After securing a nearside Chickenwing, run a Half Nelson on the far side (6:55). Staying on the near side, straighten your arm and stack him onto his shoulders (6:56). Stay on your knees and post your head for stability.

Double Chickenwing

(6:57)   **(6:58)**

(6:59)   **(6:60)**

After securing a Chickenwing on one side, secure another on the opposite side (6:57). Some coaches prefer to cross the wrists and grab the opposite triceps for security. Sit out to your inside hip, pull back to make him arch his back to prevent counter action. (6:58) As you lower him to the mat, drive toward his far shoulder, step over with your outside foot (6:59), and pivot to your head. Sit through to your inside hip and pull hard on both arms as you lean back into his hips bowing his back (6:60).

Headlever Series

The Headlever may be performed immediately after the whistle, but works best after the opponent's initial move has been stopped. Drop your outside hand to your opponent's wrist as you put the top of your head behind his arm pit. Pull the arm directly back as you pull him down to the mat with a Tight Waist.

Headlever to Half

(6:61)

(6:62)

(6:63)

(6:64)

(6:65)

With the Headlever and Tight Waist secure, duck your head under his arm maintaining control of his wrist (6:61). As you sit to your inside hip, pull downward on his wrist (6:62), but raise his upper body by leaning back (6:63). Rotate to both knees (6:64), shoot a deep half (6:65), and drive him to his back.

Head Lever to Double-Double

(6:66)

Once you have raised his upper body as previously described, quickly rotate to both knees, sink your half and secure the two-on-one (6:66) for a Double-Double, and turn him to his back. Staying on your toes and squeezing hard will create tremedous pressure on his chest.

Head Lever with Underhook to a Tulsa Pin

(6:67)

(6:68)

(6:69)

(6:70)

After securing the Headlever and far side Underhook, sit out and place your opponent's wrist on your outside hip (6:67). Post your inside foot, hold his wrist tightly to your hip, and step over him with your outside foot (6:68). Sit through as previously directed (6:69) and hold both arms securely (6:70).

Fake Tulsa to Hip Heist

(6:71)

(6:72)

(6:73)

(6:74)

As you drive around toward the Tulsa, stop (6:71), scissor your legs and rotate to your stomach (6:72, 6:73). Jerk back hard on his arms and sit through controlling both arms (6:74).

Rib Crusher

(6:75)

(6:76)

(6:77)

(6:78)

(6:79)

From the Headlever and Tight Waist, pull the opponent's arm to his hip. Reach across underneath and grab his triceps (6:75). Bend his arm to ninety degrees, post your outside knee on his wrist (6:76), and change your grip to a 'thumb up' position (6:77). Jump across his body (6:78), straighten your arm (6:79) and turn your forearm down hard into his ribs.

Rib Crusher to Stack

(6:80)　　　　　　　　　　　(6:81)

To stack the opponent, stay on his near side. After securing his wrist with your knee, use your straight arm (holding his triceps) as a lever to stack him on his shoulders (6:80, 6:81). Your knee should be behind his hips for added support and additional pressure.

Hammerlock Series

(6:82)　　　　　　　　　　　(6:83)

(6:84)

The key to the hammerlock is pressure. From a two-on-one or two-on-two, drive forward with your arms straight rolling your knuckles underneath (6:82). Lay on your opponent to keep him on his stomach. Drive your near elbow forward on his triceps, post your outside foot and scissor your legs by throwing your inside foot back over your outside foot (6:83). Stay on your toes, reach underneath his body and grab his fingers tightly with your free hand. Be sure to keep all your pressure concentrated on his triceps. Pull his arm from underneath and drive it across his back to a ninety degree angle position (6:84). Cover his arm with your body.

Several options are now available for you to turn him to his back.

Hammerlock to Baseball Bat

(6:85)

(6:86)

With the hammerlock secured, drive your opponent's wrist at a forty-five degree angle toward his hips and him toward his back (6:85). Release your grip once he reaches his side, slide your near hand underneath his arm, and shoot a Half Nelson with your outside hand (6:86).

Hammerlock to Thread Needle

(6:87)

(6:88)

(6:89)

From the Hammerlock position, use your outside elbow to reverse crossface your opponent. (6:87) As his shoulder raises, slip your hand underneath his biceps and grab his wrist (6:88). Be sure to maintain downward pressure. Walk on your knees toward his head, reach around his neck, lift his upper body (6:89), and whip him to his back.

Hammerlock to Thread Needle to Reverse Whip Over

(6:90)

(6:91)

(6:92)

The Reverse Whip Over becomes an option when the opponent braces to keep from being whipped over to his back. Once he resists, step up with your outside foot (6:90) and whip him in a reverse direction to his back (6:91). Some wrestlers prefer to hook both legs and arch in what is frequently referred to as the 'Saturday Night Ride' (6:92).

Hammerlock to Triceps Pinch Tilt

(6:93)

(6:94)

(6:95)

From the Hammerlock position, raise your upper body, scoot your outside knee forward and place it on the triceps (6:93). Release your grip with your inside hand and under hook his far shoulder (6:94), elbow deep. Step up, push off your foot and pull him to a nearfall position (6:95) holding his shoulder tightly. The wrist grip prevents him from turning toward you; the shoulder grip stops him from turning away.

The Cradle Series

As with the Crossbody, the Cradle is a great 'equalizer of men'. Many supposedly 'superior' wrestlers have been caught (or placed) in Cradles. Placing an opponent's knee near his nose makes it difficult for him to be very aggressive. A versatile move, cradles can be applied from the near side or far side, to the top leg or bottom leg, and even when the opponent is flat on his stomach. Cradles consist of one arm around the opponent's head and one around his knee with your hands locked.

There are two ideal situations for applying a cradle; when the opponent stands up (with either leg) without hand control and late in a match when the wrestler tires and drops his head.

Near Side Cradle

Bottom Leg (Basket)

(6:96)

(6:97)

(6:98)

(6:99)

(6:100)

After reaching over the opponent's head and around his knee, lock your hands (6:96). Place the top of your head in his ribs (6:97), spring forward (frog hop) pushing him to his side. (6:98) Be sure to bring your knees forward and underneath your hips. Raise his top leg, step over the bottom leg, dig your heel into the mat. Pull your heel toward you to scoop his leg, figure four his leg (6:99), and fall over his head to your side (6:100). Pull your elbows together and keep the Figure Four held tightly.

Top Leg (Roach Motel)

(6:101)

(6:102)

(6:103)

(6:104)

As you reach for the bottom leg, the opponent frequently kicks it back or away (6:101). This sets up the top leg cradle. Use your chest to push down on his top leg and step over it with your back knee. Next, step over with the front knee and sit to your inside hip (6:102). Use your thigh to push his leg to your hip (6:103). With a giant step around his head, place your forehead on the mat and stay on your toes to form a tripod (6:104) Keep your weight out toward his ankle region rather than near his hips for better leverage and a tighter pin. We referred to the top leg cradle as the 'Roach Motel' because, as the old commercial said, "When they check in, they don't check out".

Near Side Reverse Cradle

(6:105)

(6:106)

(6:107)

As the defensive wrestler steps up with his inside foot without hand control, raise your hips and reach around his neck with your inside (around his waist) hand. Reach behind his near leg with your outside arm and lock your hands (6:105). Slowly, rock him back into a cradle (6:106, 6:107). Rocking him back too quickly can lead to his flipping over you placing you on your back.

Far Side Cradle

(6:108)

(6:109)

(6:110)

As the defensive wrestler steps up with his outside foot without hand control, raise your hips and reach around his neck with your outside (on his elbow) hand. Reach behind his far leg with your inside arm and lock your hands (6:108) Step across (6:109) and slowly, rock him back into a cradle (6:110). Rocking him back too fast can lead to his flipping over you and catching you on your back. Keeping your toes under his far leg forces him to his shoulders.

Crossface Cradle

(6:111)

(6:112)

(6:113)

(6:114)

With your opponent broken down flat on the mat, secure some form of leg control. Fork his far elbow to post it as you use your wrist across his cheek to cross face him. Grab his upper arm near his shoulder and press your shoulder toward your wrist to 'squeeze the pumpkin' (6:111). Post your inside hand behind his knee and using your legs, drive his head toward his knee. Maintain your crossface and grab your own wrist (6:112). Sit to your outside hip and rock him slowly across your thigh to his back (6:113). Lift his far ankle with your top leg. If he kicks, allow him to do so, but scissor it on the way down and arch your hips into him (6:114). With the crossface held tightly, extend your arms to create even more pressure.

Crossface Cradle w/ Deadlift

(6:115)

(6:116)

(6:117)

Caught in a Crossface Cradle, opponents often turn down hard to prevent you from rocking them to their back. In this situation, step your foot between his legs with your leg bent at a ninety degree angle (6:115). Deadlift him straight up (6:116), fall to your side and his leg is automatically scissored (6:117), and extend your arms as you arch your hips and work for the pin.

Crossbody Series

The Crossbody Series requires repeated drill beginning early in your career. Also called the Grapevine, the Crossbody Series can easily control a stronger and quicker opponent because of the difficulty they have in countering it.

Farside Half

(6:118)

The Half Nelson on the far side is a frequently used technique to turn the opponent from a cross body position. Place your outside elbow on the back of his neck, reach under his far arm with your inside arm and lock your hands (6:118). Arching back, raise your elbow as you press downward on his neck and pull him to his back. Dig your other heel into his crotch to prevent him from turning away.

Reverse Crossface Scoop

(6:119)

(6:120)

(6:121)

After applying the Crossbody, place the elbow of your outside arm against the defensive man's cheekbone and push back (6:119). Reach around both your opponent's arm at the triceps level and scoop them together (6:120). Wrap both your arms around his arms, push off your foot and pull him toward his back (6:121). Dig your other heel into his crotch to prevent him from turning away.

Banana Split

(6:122)

(6:123)

(6:124)

From the Crossbody Ride, reach back and grab his far ankle with your inside hand (6:122). Reach through his crotch and grab your own wrist. Post your inside foot, push off, and pull hard on his ankle, rocking him to his back (6:123) Split his crotch, but only to hold him in position (6:124). The official will stop the move if he deems it too painful or your opponent yells out.

Guillotine

(6:125)

(6:126)

(6:127)

(6:128)

A legendary move, numerous statues have been created of the guillotine in action. From the Crossbody Ride, reach under the opponent's far arm, hook his elbow, and grab his wrist (6:125). Pull the arm back and place it behind your head, maintaining your grip on his wrist (6:126)

Reach around his head (elbow deep), push off your inside foot, arch back and fall to your side (6:127). After you meet nearfall criteria, it is permissible to lock your hands. Lock your hands above his ear and pull hard as you arch into your opponent (6:128). It is impossible for him to bridge if his head is sideways.

Double Crossbody Series

The Double Crossbody Series is very similar to the Crossbody Series. The only difference is the other leg is also applying a Crossbody Ride to the opposite leg.

Reverse Double Crossface

(6:129)

(6:130)

(6:131)

With both legs in a Crossbody position (6:129), place the elbow of your outside arm against the defensive man's cheekbone and push back (6:130). Reach around both your opponent's arm at the triceps level and scoop them together. Wrap both your arms around his arms, arch back and pull him to a nearfall position (6:131).

Half Nelson (Near side or Far side)

(6:132)

(6:133)

(6:134)

(6:135)

Regardless of the side chosen for the half, the technique is the same since both his legs are trapped identically. Reach under either arm (6:132), rotate your arm and straighten your elbow (6:133). As you drive him toward his back, release your leg holds, allowing him to turn with the pressure (6:134.) Once he is on his back, sink the half deep, and secure the Reverse Double Crossbody or as it is called in the South, the Saturday Night Ride (6:135). Arch your back, spread your legs, and pull his head up off the mat by raising your elbow.

¾ Nelson

The ¾ Nelson is named so because of it similarity to the illegal Full Nelson.

After breaking your opponent down with a tight waist and arm chop, hook his near leg, raise up to release pressure from his back, and allow him to 'base up'. Three possible options to completing the ¾ are available.

"Hey Mama" 1 Over-1 Under

(6:136)

(6:137)

(6:138)

(6:139)

The "Hey Mama" label was developed as a learning cue for the top man's hand position (6:136). Reaching underneath the opponent with your near hand, place your wrist directly beside the outer portion of his neck. The palm is facing forward as to wave at 'Mama' in the bleachers. Reach over the opponent's near shoulder and neck, and lock your hands (6:137). Pull your elbows downward and toward each other squeezing tightly. Keeping his leg locked, pull him directly over to his shoulders for the pin (6:138, 6:139).

"Hey Mama" Both Under

(6:140)

(6:141)

The ¾ Nelson, with both arms underneath is more difficult to secure. Rather than reaching over the opponent's shoulder, reach underneath and lock your hands in a position similar to a full nelson (6:140). Pull your elbows down and toward each other. Keeping his leg locked, pull him directly over to his shoulders for the pin (6:141).

Knee Option

(6:142)

(6:143)

(6:144)

With the tremendous strength possessed by many of today's wrestlers, it is often difficult to pull the opponent directly forward to his back. As an option, lower your inside shoulder and place it in his ribs (6:142). Pull his head toward your outside knee, (6:143) fall to your side dragging his leg around and Figure 4 it. (6:144) Pull your elbows together to tighten the lock.

Barbed Wire

(6:145)

(6:146)

(6:147)

(6:148)

(6:149)

Barbed Wire begins with a cross face while the opponent is on his base (6:145). Reach underneath his body with your inside arm and grab his far elbow slightly below the cross face hand (6:146) Pull his trapped arms with your arms and push to his side with your upper body (6:147) As he lays on his side, walk around his head clockwise (holding both his arms) to turn him to his back (6:148).Scoop his head laterally to prevent a bridge.(6:149)

Garner Roll Variations

As previously discussed, the Garner Roll may be used to 'kill the clock', but with ample time remaining, may be used as a pinning combination to earn a nearfall.

Underneath Garner

(6:150)

(6:151)

(6:152)

With the head locked and your foot hooked by your opponent, step up and post your outside foot. To create momentum, drop to your shoulder, duck your head underneath (6:150), jerk the headlock and roll through (across your back) taking your opponent to his back (6:151). Lift the trapped leg and squeeze tightly on the headlock (6:152). Note: If the opponent begins to escape, 'base out' and 'belly down' to maintain control.

Over The Top

(6:153)

(6:154)

(6:155)

When defensive wrestlers are locked in the Garner Roll position, they often pull in the opposite direction to prevent the roll through pin (6:153). When this occurs, an excellent option is available. As the opponent pulls away, use his pressure to your advantage. Step up with your outside leg (6:154), push off your foot hard and take him in the direction he is pressuring. Post your free foot to stop the momentum. Lift the trapped leg and squeeze tightly on the headlock (6:155).

Turkey Bar Stack

(6:156)

(6:157)

After securing the Turkey Bar Ride, slide your inside knee directly in front of your opponent (6:156). Pull downward on the arm and lifting up on his hips with your arm and thigh, drive him forward to stack him on his shoulders (6:157) Sitting through and leaning back places tremendous pressure on his back and makes avoiding the pin almost impossible.

CHAPTER 7

Escapes and Reversals

Bottom Position

(7:1)   (7:2)

For optimum success, proper position when on bottom is essential. The standard position includes; sitting on your feet (to prevent your opponent from grabbing an ankle), your weight back (off your hands), head up, your hands directly in front of your knees, and your arms slightly bent inward (7:1). Bending the arms and forcing your elbows outward provides 'hooks' for your opponent and should be avoided.

Note: In you are involved in heavyweight competition; your back should be arched to prevent the offensive wrestler from placing his weight on you to prevent movement (7:2).

Changeover

(7:3)   **(7:4)**

The Changeover is a technique used to move or 'change' your opponent from one side (usually your weak side) to the other where you are more competent. It can be extremely valuable to the beginning or inexperienced wrestler who has not developed skill from both sides.

Raise your inside knee without moving the foot, pull the near elbow to your raised knee (7:3), slap your hand on the mat near your hip (7:4), and return to your base. The movement has forced the opponent to 'change over' to the opposite side. The Changeover can be beneficial in two ways. First, it can be used to change your opponent over from your weak side to your strong side. Secondly, it can force your opponent to change over from his strong side to his weaker side giving you an advantage.

Standup

Without a doubt, the Standup is the most widely used escape maneuver at all levels of competition. An explosive move, it is difficult to stop and should be the first bottom technique taught. The Standup has a tremendous success rate, is a versatile move, and provides several options and 'second moves' after you reach your feet.

Teaching the Standup:

(7:5)

(7:6)

(7:7)

(7:8)

(7:9)

(7:10)

(7:11)   **(7:12)**

Step1 (7:5) Using your wrists, spring up off your hands and raise your hips off your feet. (Repeat 5-6 times).

Step 2 (7:6) Spring up off your hands, raise off your feet, and step up placing your foot directly in front at a 90 degree angle.(Repeat 5-6 times).

Step 3 (7:7) Spring up off your hands, raise off your feet, step up placing your foot directly in front at a 90 degree angle, and pull your inside elbow back toward your side firmly, with your fist clinched and your palm facing upward. As the palm rotates upward, the elbow is forced toward your side. It is imperative that your elbow be held very tightly to your side. This closes the space and prevents your opponent from locking his hands. (Repeat 5-6 times)

Step 4 (7:8) Spring up off your hands, raise off your feet, step up placing your foot directly in front at a 90 degree angle, and pull your inside elbow back toward your side firmly, with your fist clinched and your palm facing upward. With your other hand, grab your imaginary opponent's fingers and squeeze tightly. While drilling, grabbing one's t-shirt reinforces the grasping action (Repeat 5-6 times).

Step 5 Maintaining the Step 4 position, keep your feet as they are, keep your hips low and pivot up to both feet. (Repeat 5-6 times)

Step 6 From position 5, pull the imaginary hand off your stomach (7:9), 'put it in your pocket' (7:10) (place it behind your outside hip), and walk away from your imaginary opponent (7:11) to escape. Be sure to maintain your grip on his fingers and a proper stance until you are free from his grasp (7:12) (Repeat 5-6 times).

Step 7 Slowly go through the entire move 5-6 times and gradually increase speed.

Standups must be a part of every practice! NO exceptions!

Second Moves (Re-establish Base drill)

(7:13)   (7:14)

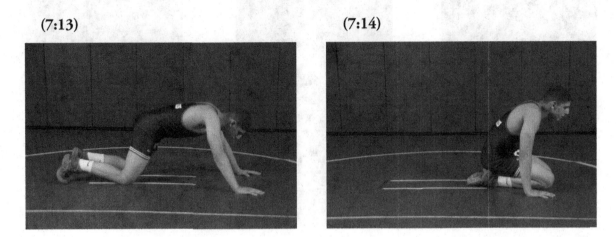

Sometimes the opponent is quicker than you are and stops your standup by driving forward and chopping your near arm. No Problem! Put your weight on your hands (7:13), scoot your knees forward re-establish your base (7:14), then execute the standup. This action may be drilled successfully, with or without a partner.

Standup Second Moves

Things don't always go as planned and on occasions, the offensive wrestler may secure a waist lock after you are standing. Several options are available that have proven to be successful when properly executed. All the second moves require securing a two-on-one grip on his outside wrist (the one opposite the side his head is on). It is imperative to stay in a good stance with our knees bent, your head up, and your feet shoulder width apart.

Dariel W. Daniel

Standing Switch

(7:15)  (7:16)  (7:17)

The Standing Switch begins from a standing position with your knees bent and a 2 on 1 grip on his outside forearm. (7:15) Release your grip with your outside hand and reach to his inner thigh (7:16) and slowly walk away from your opponent putting tremendous pressure on his shoulder. As his grip is broken, complete the Basic Switch (7:17) to complete the reversal.

Falling Switch

(7:18)

(7:19)

144

(7:20)

Considered by many (including me) to be one of the more powerful moves in wrestling, the Falling Switch is nearly unstoppable. The Falling Switch begins as you release your grip on his wrist with your inside hand (nearest his head) and fall directly forward (7:18). As you near the mat, post your inside hand on the mat and release your grip on his wrist. With your outside foot remaining in place, pivot your hips completely through. As you are pivoting, bend your arm completely, clinch your fist, and concentrate all your power into his shoulder (7:19) as you fall powerfully to your hip breaking him down. Circle behind your opponent to complete the reversal. (7:20)

Dragging a foot (pretending to trip) and stumbling as you move forward (as if you are stumbling) extends your opponent's arms and makes the move even more devastating.

Standing Wayne Roll

(7:21)

(7:22)

(7:23)

(7:24)

(7:25)

Part of the Granby System, the Wayne Roll is effective from the standing position, as well as down on the mat. When properly executed, it results in a reversal, nearfall, and potentially, a pin.

Lower your level (7:21), release your grip with your inside hand, and place it behind your opponent's outside knee (palm down, thumb up) (7:22). Drop to your outside knee (7:23), then your elbow (7:24) while maintaining a tight grip on wrist. Throw his leg backward forcing him onto his back. Immediately after throwing his far leg, switch in midair to his near leg. Secure a two-on-one grip on his secured wrist to complete the reversal.(7:25)

Standing Peterson Roll

(7:26)

(7:27)

(7:28)

The Standing Peterson Roll requires a 'fake switch' motion to get your opponent to step around. As he steps around, lower your level and step behind his near leg (7:26) hooking it with your inside arm. Drop to your outside knee, then to your elbow (7:27) while maintaining a tight grip on his wrist, keeping your head up and completing the roll. Secure a two-on-one grip on the controlled wrist to complete the reversal (7:28).

Step Behind Setback

(7:29)

The Setback requires a 'fake switch' motion to get the opponent to step around. As he steps around, lower your level and quickly step behind his near leg (7:29) hooking it with your inside arm. Push back hard into his stomach and sit to your inside hip, Secure a two-on-one grip on the controlled wrist to complete the reversal and work for the nearfall or pin.

The Whip

(7:30) **(7:31)**

The Whip is a little-known move that almost guarantees an escape or reversal. Release your grip with your outside hand, extend your arm backwards (7:30), step back and block your opponent's foot. Next, throw your extended arm 'down and away' in a whipping motion. With his foot blocked, your opponent will be tripped and fall to his side (7:31). Release your grip on his wrist, turn to your stomach and quickly 'cover' him.

Standing Whizzer/ Standing Hiplock

(7:32) **(7:33)** **(7:34)**

Due to being on your feet rather than on the knees, the Standing Whizzer is slightly different from the one on the mat. With your outside hand, fake a switch (7:32) to get the opponent to step around in the opposite direction. Rotate your feet 90 degrees toward your opponent (7:33), as you over hook his arm. Rotate your upper body clockwise creating shoulder pressure to make him step forward. As he steps forward, step around and face him for an escape (7:34).

The Sitout Series

The Sitout can be used to escape or set up a second move. The Long Sitout is used primarily to escape, while the Short Sitout sets other moves up as you remain very close to your opponent's legs. The Sitout begins with raising the outside knee off the mat and sitting to your inside hip. Only raise your knee far enough off the mat to allow you to sit your leg underneath it. The distance the leg is extended determines whether the Sitout is considered long or short. Regardless of the type Sitout used, it is imperative to keep your head in front of your hips to prevent the offensive man from jerking you to your back.

Long

(7:35)

(7:36)

(7:37)

The Long Sitout requires you to sit your extended leg far out and directly in front of you (7:35). Drop to your inside shoulder hard, as you kick your outside leg over to the mat creating momentum (7:36). Post your outside hand on the mat and throw your inside hand up (7:37), to prevent your opponent from following behind you. Often, opponents are caught in 'midair' attempting to follow behind.

Short

(7:38)   **(7:39)**

The Short Sitout is used primarily as preliminary action to set up a secondary move. Raise your outside knee (7:38) as you secure wrist control. Sit your inside leg directly in front of you (7:39) and look for a second move.

Peterson Roll

(7:40)

After a Short Sitout (7:40), turn inward and hook the opponent's near leg with your arm (elbow deep). Thrust your outside elbow forward and, keeping your head up, drop to your outside hip rolling him to his back. Secure a two-on-one grip and work for a nearfall or fall.

Wayne Roll

After a Short Sitout, turn inward and hook the opponent's far knee from the inside. With your arm elbow deep pull his leg in toward your body.

Maintaining your grip on his wrist, scoot your outside knee forward, drop to your hip, and thrust your elbow forward while keeping your head up. Throw his leg over your back forcing him to his back. Immediately after throwing his far leg, switch in midair to his near leg. Secure a two-on-one grip on his secured wrist to complete the reversal

Guizzonne

(7:41)

(7:42)

(7:43)

The Guizzone is a moved designed for a very specific situation. If, after a Sitout, your opponent reaches over your shoulder, grab his wrist securely with the opposite hand (7:41). Hook his upper arm with your elbow, fall to your shoulder as you complete the turn (7:42), escape and face your opponent.(7:43)

Headhook

(7:44)

(7:45)

(7:46)

The Headhook is a moved designed for a very specific situation. After a Sitout, if the opponent places his head over your shoulder, hook his head securely with the same side arm (7:44). Fall to your shoulder forcefully as you complete the turn (7:45), face your opponent and escape. Some coaches prefer the wrestler to 'swim' his head underneath his opponent's arm (7:46) and drive him directly to his back.

Granby Roll

(7:47)

(7:48)

(7:49)

Once the Short Sitout is completed, maintain wrist control. Push off your outside foot, throw your inside arm behind you (7:47). As you roll across the top of your shoulders, grab the opponent's leg tightly (7:48). Once the roll is completed, you will be in the two-on-one position (7:49) with reversal points forthcoming and possibly, a nearfall. The Granby variations are a very complicated series and require daily drilling to be proficient in even the basics.

Switch

The Switch is one of the older moves in wrestling. Appropriately named, the Switch allows wrestlers to 'switch 'places and earns the defensive wrestler a reversal. Recently, there has been a movement toward a more modern version of the Basic Switch where the inside thigh is not grabbed. In addition, the Inside Switch and Power Switch are extremely effective because of the leverage involved. Note: In all Switch drills, the coach must instruct the drill partner to keep his arm around his partner's waist. Attempting to pull the arm out transfers the pressure to the top man's elbow, and can result in a hyperextension.

Basic (old) Switch

(7:50) **(7:51)**

(7:52) **(7:53)**

(7:54)

The Basic (old) Switch begins as you rotate your palm upward to free your arm (7:50) and move your near elbow toward the far elbow. As you post your hand on the mat be sure is far enough away that your opponent can't reach it (7:51), raise your outside knee without moving your foot (7:52), and pivot your hips completely through (7:53). As you are pivoting, focus all your power into his shoulder as you rotate powerfully to your hip and grab inside his thigh. By keeping your arm extended, pressuring the shoulder, and rotating to your hip, his base is destroyed. Circle behind your opponent to complete the reversal. (7:54)

Modern Switch

(7:55)

The Modern Switch begins as you quickly rotate your palm upward to free your arm and move your near elbow to the far elbow. Post your inside hand on the mat (far enough away that your opponent can't reach it). Without moving your outside foot, raise your outside knee, and pivot your hips completely through until you are on your inside hip and applying pressure to his shoulder. Maintain a bent arm and clinched fist (7:55). The pressure destroys his base and flattens him out. Circle behind your opponent to complete the reversal.

This Modern Switch basically eliminates all counters.

Inside Switch

(7:56)

(7:57)

(7:58)

The Inside Switch begins with a quick two-hand fake to the outside freeing your inside arm. Reach over your opponent's arm as you raise your inside knee (7:56) and grab inside his thigh (7:57). Sit hard to your inside hip creating tremendous pressure on his shoulder to break him down off his base. Circle behind your opponent to complete the reversal (7:58).

Power Switch

(7:59)

(7:60)

(7:61)

The Power Switch begins with a quick two-hand fake to the outside freeing your inside arm. Reach over your opponent's arm as you raise your inside knee and place your clinched fist underneath it (7:59). Sit hard to your inside hip (7:60) as you extend your leg to kick his knee outward. Placing all the pressure in his shoulder joint forces him to collapse from his base. (7:61) Circle behind your opponent to complete the reversal.

Throwby

(7:62)

(7:63)

(7:64)

The Throwby is not a widely used or frequently available option. It is, however, a move that you should know for the rare occasions it is available. With the opponent's knee close to your body, reach back and grab his leg by the shin (7:62). Pivot your inside leg up (7:63), throw his leg away from you (7:64), and then sit out for an escape.

Whizzer (Hiplock)

(7:65)

(7:66)

The Whizzer (or Hiplock) is primarily know as a defensive technique, but can be used as an offensive move as well. It is very effective when used to escape, but has many secondary moves that lead to reversals and/or pins. These include the ¼ Nelson, Headlock, Whipover, and Lateral Drop.

The basic offensive Whizzer begins with three simultaneous movements. The outside foot rotates outward as a post; the arm rotates upward in a windmill fashion to grab the inside of your thigh (over hooking his arm) as your inside knee pivots up (without moving your foot).(7:65)

In a 'down and around' motion, pull his shoulder toward the mat (7:66). Kick your leg up, arch your back during the power rotation, and kick your leg free on the way down. Sit to your near hip, turn and face your opponent maintaining the over hook position. The escape has been completed.

Stepover Arm Cradle

(7:67)

The Stepover Arm Cradle can be executed when the rotating action flattens your opponent, but your leg is still trapped. Maintain the arm over hook, step up with your outside foot, push backwards, and post your foot behind you (7:67). Be sure to remain bent over from the waist, keep your head in front, place your hand under his near leg, and lock your hands to complete a Stepover Arm Cradle.

Stepover Cradle

The Stepover Cradle is a surprising and effective move, especially for the upper weight class wrestlers. Without looking, cross your inside leg over your opponent's far leg and post your toe firmly on the mat. Quickly pull your hands closer to your knees, and pop your hips high into the air. Backing into your opponent, step back over and post your foot flatly on the mat keeping you knee bent at a 90 degree angle.

Reach under his near leg and grab your own thigh. Raise your elbow to create pressure. After securing control, reach around his neck and lock your hands in a cradle.

Note: If your opponent reacts quickly as you change your foot, and moves away from you, turn your foot sideways and execute the Basic Sitout.

Wing Roll

(7:68)

(7:69)

(7:70)

The Wing Roll can be done 'right off the whistle', but is most effective after a Sitout due to the momentum created by your motion.

Grab the wrist that is around your waist, slide both your knees together, toward, and underneath your opponent (7:68). The concept of being a 'beachball' should be emphasized to imply it is almost impossible for your opponent to prevent the roll. Maintaining your grip on his wrist, throw your elbow forward and around as you drop to your outside hip (7:69). Kick your opponent over, hook his near leg with your arm, and secure a two-on-one position to complete the reversal.(7:70)

Crosswrist Wingroll

(7:71)

(7:72)

(7:73)

The Crosswrist Roll is, as the name implies, a variation of the basic Wingroll. With your inside hand, reach across and grab the wrist of the arm around your waist. Slide your knees together, toward, and underneath your opponent (7:71). Throw your outside elbow forward as you drop to your outside hip (7:72). Kick him over, hook his near leg with your arm, grab his outside wrist with your outside hand and secure a two-on-one to complete the reversal.(7:73)

CHAPTER 8

Takedowns From Behind

The Most Neglected Area of Technique

The most neglected and under-coached area of wrestling technique without a doubt has to be 'takedowns from behind'. I really can't decide if coaches are just weak in technique from this position or feel that it is not really that important. It is very important if you want your kids to become champions. We've all seen close matches where the offensive wrestler is standing behind the defensive wrestler and pulls him back of top of himself. Drilling on takedowns from behind a minimum of twice a week will solve this problem.

Basically, when you are behind someone in a standing position four things can happen and three are not good:

1. Your opponent may escape. (BAD)

2. Your opponent may execute a standing reversal. (BAD)

3. You may be warned or penalized for stalling. (BAD)

4. You may successfully return him to the mat. (GOOD)

Points to Remember:

1. The longer your opponent stays on his feet, the more the odds favor his being successful in executing an escape or reversal move. Take him down IMMEDIATELY!

2. His hip must be posted on almost every takedown from behind.

3. You, as the offensive wrestler, are responsible for your opponent's safe return to the mat.

Proper Position When Standing Behind the Opponent

Position in any technique is important, but in takedowns from behind, it is crucial. The correct position of the head, hands, and feet prior to executing any takedown must be attained. (8:1)

Hands

The hands are used to post the opponent's feet. They must be locked using the thumb grab or pinkie grip on either side. The palm of the deepest arm is turned down. Pushing the lower forearm into the hip joint hard posts his feet so they can't move. With a posted hip, your opponent is unable to execute any offensive move. The hip is posted on EVERY takedown from behind.

Head

The head is placed near the hands. The importance of this position is two-fold. First, it enables you to see his feet and secondly, it prevents any reach backs and hip tosses.

Feet

(8:1)

The feet are approximately two feet (no pun intended) behind and parallel to your opponent's feet. (8:1)

Now you are ready!

TEN TAKEDOWNS FROM BEHIND

Lift and Tilt

(8:2)   (8:3)

The Lift and Tilt is probably the most commonly used of all the variations. After getting into proper position, hop forward placing your hips under his hips; raise your hips to lift him off the mat (8:2). Cut your arm into his hip swinging his legs parallel (8:3) to the mat and drop to cover him (8:3).

It must be a quick, smooth, and forceful action. The knee tap varies only in the fact that after he is lifted, rather than cutting his hip with your elbow, you stand like a crane on one foot, swing your knee laterally and knock his legs parallel to the mat.

Back Heel—Face Kick

(8:4)   (8:5)

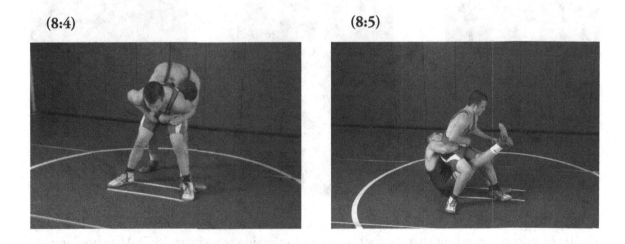

(8:6)

The back heel has evolved through the years into a safe and solid move. In the 'old days', wrestlers stepped on the back of both heels. Later, coaches decided it was safer to just step on one heel. Now we step on one heel and kick the other leg between his legs and toward his face. The progression was a slow and costly process (in terms of mistakes), but now it is safe and reliable.

After posting his feet, look at the nearside heel, turn your foot sideways and post it on his heel as you lower your hips (8:4) Quickly pull him back and to the side as you simultaneously kick your other foot up between his legs toward his face (8:5). Although it is almost impossible to do, the 'kick him in the face' expression delivers the concept quite nicely. Once the move is completed, he will be on his side, you'll be on top, and your leg will be between his legs preventing all switches (8:6). It is important as a learning technique to visualize every inch of the side of your leg touching the mat.

As a learning tool, lower your hips to an exaggerated level before completing the move to get the feeling of touching all parts of the side of the leg. I say "Pretend there is a piece of tape on the side of your leg and you want to put it all flat on the mat".

Front Trip or Outside Trip

(8:7)   **(8:8)**   **(8:9)**

After posting his feet, lower your hips and hook his ankle with your knee. The action is very similar to a drop step except that the foot is turned to the side as you step (8:7) After hooking his ankle and pressing forward with your chest (8:8), use your hand around his waist to sling him laterally (8:9). After slinging him, sit back on the hooked ankle and pull your arm up. Falling on top of him only invites a switch or roll.

T-Bar to a Turk

(8:10)   **(8:11)**   **(8:12)**

After posting his feet, quickly hop to the side opposite where your hands are locked. At the same time you will release your grip, reach through his crotch and lock your hand onto your forearm forming a T (8:10). Since you are still squatting, it will be easy to lift him off the mat by straightening your legs. Allow the far leg to drop to the mat, along with his head (8:11). Step through, hooking his leg (8:12), drop step to your front knee into a Turk position.

Drop and Tackle

(8:13)   **(8:14)**

The Drop and Tackle move is primarily for heavyweights, but can be used by lighter wrestlers as a last resort. It, as the name states, involves dropping to your knees and tackling him from behind. After posting his feet, drop to your knees, grab both of his shins (or ankles), drive your shoulder into the back of the knees and push forward (8:13). After he drops to his knees (8:14), immediately move up and break your opponent down.

Foot Sweep

(8:15)   **(8:16)**   **(8:17)**

The Foot Sweep is the most complicated of all the moves from this position. It requires perfect timing and repeated drill. After posting his feet, release your grip, grab his outside ankle as you drop to your outside knee (8:15). Simultaneously, you must pull on his far hip to transfer his weight to the near foot (8:16). As you pull the near ankle backwards hard, you must 'foot sweep' his far ankle (8:17). It takes repeated practice, but is a smooth move.

Foot Smash

(8:18)   **(8:19)**

The Foot Smash is the second 'primarily' heavyweight move of the series. After posting his feet, step around and place your foot directly on top of his foot (8:18). It is now posted even more than before. Keep your weight on his foot and push him forward until he falls to the mat (8:19). It's not really complicated, but works well with the 'big boys'.

The following three takedowns are also executed from behind your opponent. (also called Rear Standing Position) start with your opponent standing with near arm tied up in a Cross Wrist Ride situation. By being 'tied up', we mean that you have the wrist and elbow of the near arm tightly secured.

Standing Heard Roll

(8:20)   **(8:21)**   **(8:22)**

With the arm tied up, push your opponent forward to make him step. When he steps with his far foot, release your near hand grip (8:20), reach under his far thigh and hook his leg with your hand and wrist. As you fall to your outside knee, jerk simultaneously on his wrist and waist (8:21). Your opponent will fall to his back in a nearfall position. Hold his wrist and thigh tightly as you work for a pin (8:22).

Scissor Setback

(8:23)

The Scissor Setback is a simple, but effective move. With the arm tied up, step around and place your outside foot behind his far thigh. Straighten the leg (as in a prying position) as you pull back on his elbow and wrist sitting him to the mat (8:23).

Knee Setback

(8:24)

The Knee Setback is an old move from the 1960's, but it still has value if used properly. From the standing position with the arm tied up, release your grip on the elbow, lower your level and hook his knee with your outside arm. Pull the wrist hard as you raise your outside arm taking him to his back (8:24).

Takedown From Behind If He Grabs Your Leg

Swim Foot to Back Heel

On the occasions where an opponent reaches back between his own legs and grabs your leg, DO NOT PANIC! Swim the foot of the grabbed leg to the outside of his leg. This movement makes it impossible for your opponent to pull it forward. Once the foot is outside, execute the Back Heel move previously discussed. The only difference is you are just kicking the leg up hard on the outside rather than toward his face. Hit the move immediately after swimming the foot outside and before he releases his grip.

Deciding Which Takedown From Behind to Use

It makes a difference which takedown from behind you use in certain situations. Some are designed to use when the opponent is standing still, some are to be used if he is moving forward (as to go out of bounds) and others if he is pushing backward to keep from going off the mat.

The following may be helpful in determining which to use:

Standing Still: All

Moving Forward: Heard Roll, Front Trip, Foot Smash

Moving Backward: Back Heel-Face Kick, Knee Setback, Scissor Setback

CHAPTER 9

Attacking the Top 20 Offensive Moves

While 'counter' is the most commonly used word to describe a defensive technique, I have not accepted it and do not endorse using it with middle school or high school wrestlers.

I prefer to tell wrestlers that "We don't counter, we stop our opponent's motion and then attack him" or "We put our opponent out of position and attack", or "We use our opponent's motion to our benefit in taking him down or turning him to his back". It is a state of the mind that keeps your wrestler in an offensive mode rather than always thinking defensively.

Hundreds of moves have been developed to stop a wrestler's offensive attack. There are counters, and counters to the counters, and counters to the counter's counter. A never-ending list of technique exists that increases almost daily. To be effective in scholastic wrestling, a wrestler must be able to stop the top twenty offensive moves as a minimum standard.

Takedowns

Double Leg

(9:1)

The most popular way to defend a Double Leg is to sprawl. After sprawling, several options are available. The ¼ Nelson (to Turn, Shuck, Heel, or Headlock), Double Crossface, Thigh Block, and Ankle Grab. Sprawl drills are very popular with coaches as sprawls are used in practically every match, usually more than five or six times. A sprawl is defined as 'throwing your legs back to prevent attack'. (9:1)

Sprawl Drill

(9:2)   **(9:3)**

Sprawl drills may be executed as a team or in pairs. Some coaches prefer to have the entire team to face them, chop their feet, sprawl, and circle back up to their stance, on his whistle.

I prefer a more realistic version where wrestlers are in pairs as in a match. Both wrestlers move around in their stance. One wrestler (offense) points quickly toward either leg (9:2), or sometimes both legs of the defensive wrestler. The defensive wrestler sprawls quickly to the appropriate hip (or hips) pointed at (9:3) and circles back up to a stance. After 30-45 seconds, wrestlers swap responsibilities. This forces the wrestler to react to motion toward his legs simulating a single or double leg takedown. Some wrestlers, especially beginners like to hop up and sprawl backward. Insist that their hip motion is always down and away.

Single Leg

Defensive technique for the single leg attack is basically the technique for the double leg attack, except that you sprawl to the attacked hip rather than both. Additional techniques used to stop a single leg include the Whizzer (Hiplock), Keylock, and the Spladdle.

Different technique is required if the opponent picks the leg up including the Double Crossface Stomp, Setback Cradle, Whizzer to the ¼ Nelson, and the Over-Under Lateral Drop. The position of your leg, i.e., outside, in front of your opponent, or between his legs determines the appropriate move to execute.

Single Leg on the Mat

Whizzer (Hiplock)

(9:4)

(9:5)

(9:6)

The Whizzer, also known as the Hiplock, is an effective defense for the single leg because of the angle of attack. Over hook his top arm and grab your inner thigh (9:4). Using your hips, power down on his shoulder (9:5), scoot around to face him (9:6) and move to a second maneuver.

Keylock

(9:7)

The Keylock is used after the attacker has circled around toward your ankle. Over hook his arm and grab your own ankle (9:7). Trap his arm and wait for a stalemate preventing a takedown.

Spladdle

(9:8)

(9:9)

The Spladdle catches many wrestlers by surprise as they attempt a single. It takes them from an excellent position to one directly on their back. As the offensive wrestler attacks your single leg with his head on the inside, post your attacked leg, reach over your opponent's head and arm to grab the inside of his far thigh (9:8). Pull his leg toward your body, lock your hands, sit to your near hip and dig your heel into the mat trapping his near leg. Pull the leg to your chest and keep the bottom leg tightly secured by scissoring your legs around it (9:9). The opponent goes directly to his back and begins his struggle to avoid a pin.

Single With Your Leg on the Outside

Double Crossface-Stomp

Immediately after your leg is picked up, 'swim' your foot to the outside of your opponent's inside hip. Apply a Hiplock (Whizzer) and pressure down on your opponent's shoulder. Push the side of his head away (9:10) and reach across to grab his far triceps with your inside hand (9:11). Put the top of your head on the side of your opponent's neck. Grab his far triceps with your free hand and pull hard creating pressure on his neck and shoulder (9:12). Pull upward on his arms (9:13) and stomp your foot down hard to free your leg (9:14).

Next pull both his arms under your armpit (9:15). He is now 'at your mercy' and you have three viable options for taking him to the mat: Hip Toss, Double Arm Drag, Fireman's Carry

Hip Toss

(9:16)

(9:17)

(9:18)

Holding his arms securely, pull up hard forcing him to his toes, step across with your inside leg and hit his legs above his outside knee (9:16) sweeping his legs from underneath him (9:17) and taking him to his back with both arms tied up.(9:18) Use caution when taking him to the mat as you are responsible for his safety.

Double Arm Drag

(9:19)

(9:20)

(9:21)

Another option with the Double Arm tieup is the Double Arm Drag. The first step is to use your free hand to push your opponent's head behind your inside shoulder. (9:19) Step forward with your outside foot as you drag him to the mat and sit on your hip. (9:20, 9:21). Turn immediately to your stomach and work for a pin.

Fireman's Carry

(9:22)

(9:23)

(9:24)

A third option from the Double Arm Tieup is the Fireman's Carry. With both his arms secure (9:22), swim your head underneath both his arms (9:23) and pull down tightly as you drop to both knees. As you drop, put your free arm up his crotch, pull down hard on his arms, raise off your heels and dump him to his back. (9:24)

Over-Under Lateral Drop With Your Leg on the Outside

(9:25)

(9:26)

(9:27)

A somewhat flashy move, the lateral from this position is effective if appropriate pressure is applied to the near knee. After securing the Whizzer, drop your inside foot behind his near knee (9:25). Reach across and under hook his far arm (9:26). Hop one step forward, fall to your inside hip as you kick the opponent over to his back with your foot behind his knee (9:27).

Single With your Leg In Front

Setback Cradle

(9:28)   **(9:29)**

With your leg directly in front or between his legs and a Whizzer secured, hop back one small step, bend over and grab behind your opponent's knee (9:28). As you grab the knee, kick directly back with your leg setting him on his hips. Lock your hands to secure an arm cradle (9:29).

Fireman's Carry

(9:30)   **(9:31)**

To stop a fireman's carry, sprawl to both hips, and block the opponent's inside thigh with your free arm stopping his motion (9:30). Reach back and grab his fingers, pull his hand off your leg (9:31). Switch off to a front headlock or other offensive technique.

Arm Drag

(9:32)　　　　　　　　　　　**(9:33)**

(9:34)　　　　　　　　　　　**(9:35)**

As your opponent drags your arm (9:32), stop his motion by grabbing his triceps, step forward, and re-drag him (9:33, 9:34) down to the mat. (9:35) A second technique would involve 'swimming' your arm down and around his waist as you feel the drag beginning.

Front Headlock

(9:36)

From the headlock position, you must first secure his elbow using both hands and squeezing tightly. Release your grip with the bottom hand (nearest the elbow). Drag his elbow through as you step up with your outside foot (9:36), turn you head sideways and reach over his far hip to gain control.

Headlock

Defensive technique for the 'deadly' headlock is essential. Many supposedly superior wrestlers have been pinned while holding big leads.

Re-throw From the Standing Position

(9:37)

(9:38)

(9:39)

As the opponent starts the headlock (9:37), step around with you outside foot (9:38), lock your hands, arch your back and throw him (9:39).

Headlock on the Mat

Roll Through

(9:40)

If you get thrown to your back in a headlock, remain calm. Scoot your hips toward your opponent's, lock your hands around his waist, jerk hard, bridge and roll him through (9:40) to his back.

Hip Block on The Mat

If you are unable to lock your hands around your opponent's waist while on your back, there is an alternative. Place your free hand on the mat against your opponent's near hip and gradually push it away. As his hips move away, his leverage decreases and you are able to turn to your stomach and escape the pinning situation.

Lateral Drop

Crotch Block

In an over and under position, always anticipate a Lateral Drop. As the lateral begins, lower your hips and grab his crotch taking him to his back.

Bear Hug

Double Overhook to Salto

(9:41)   **(9:42)**

With the Bear Hug firmly locked up, you must react quickly by securing double over hooks. Step between his feet, arch to your head (9:41), turn to your shoulder and sit through to complete the Salto (9:42)

Knuckles to Sternum with Headlock

(9:43)   **(9:44)**

After securing the Double Overhook, use both sets of your knuckles to press hard into your opponent's sternum (9:43). Move immediately to a staggered stance. As he moves his hips back, headlock him to the mat (9:44).

Escape and Reversal Defense

Standup

As previously stated, the standup is the most popular move from the bottom in scholastic wrestling. If your opponent is superior on his feet, you must be able to stop his standup to have a chance to win. There are two basic ways to stop the initial phase of the standup, the Bump and the Thigh Block. Both moves are designed to only stop the step up and you must immediately change off to a second move.

Bump

(9:45)

The Bump basically pushes the bottom man laterally and off his stable base. With your outside foot stepped up, push hard off the foot and with your chest into his side disrupting his technique (9:45).

Thigh Block

(9:46)

The Thigh block is extremely effective in stopping the Standup. On the whistle, release his elbow and hit his inside thigh hard with your lower arm (9:46). Immediately swap off to a breakdown or ride.

Switch

The second most popular move from the bottom is the switch. Four basic defenses to the switch (the old switch) have proven to be effective.

Re-Switch

(9:47)   (9:48)

As the bottom man reaches inside your thigh for the switch, pressure your inside knee toward his hip and keep your arm around his waist. As he leans into your shoulder, raise your inside knee (9:47), sit through to your hip and secure a rear crotch position (9:48).

Thigh Hook

(9:49)   (9:50)

(9:51)

As the switch begins, release your grip around your opponent's waist, hook his near thigh and grab the top of your own thigh (9:49). Pushing off your outside foot, drive into him hard (9:50) knocking him to his side (9:51).

Sit Through

(9:52)

Once the bottom man has reached inside your thigh, sit through to your inside hip and lean into his shoulder (9:52). It places tremendous pressure on his elbow. Turn to your knees and chop the near arm to break him down to his side. Move directly into the head lever series.

Hook and Roll

(9:53)

(9:54)

(9:55)

Basically a 'clinic' move, the Hook and Roll is fairly unknown. It is, however, very effective if drilled and executed properly. Once your opponent's hand is inside your thigh, hold his waist tightly to stop his motion (9:53). Step over his near leg, hook it with your leg, raise your hips, roll forward (9:54), scoot your hips out, secure a rear crotch hold, and go behind him for a reversal (9:55)

Granby Roll

The key to stopping any Granby Roll (standing or on the mat) is hip control. If the offensive wrestler is not able to elevate his hips for power, his Granby Roll is prevented.

Snatch Back

(9:56)

(9:57)

The first technique is used immediately after the bottom man sits out. Reach inside both sides as you push forward with the side of your head in the upper center of his back (9:56). As he presses back, reach under both arms, hook his shoulders and snatch him back underneath your chest (9:57).

Roll Through

(9:58)

With your head in the center of his back and a hand around his waist and one on his elbow, 'freeze' your body, and roll through as he rolls through (9:58). Break him down to his stomach as he reaches a sitting position.

Wingroll

Crossover

(9:59)   **(9:60)**

Immediately as you feel your opponent grab your wrist (9:59), jump to the opposite side (9:60) destroying his leverage and stopping the Wingroll.

Head in his Side

(9:61)   **(9:62)**

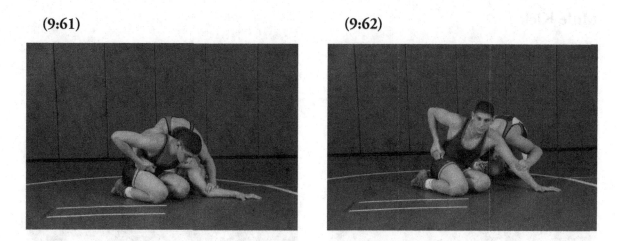

As the defensive wrestler grabs your wrist, drop your upper body downward and place the top of your head in his ribs (9:61, 9:62). This position eliminates his leverage and prevents his Wingroll.

Peterson Roll

Knee Pop

(9:63)   **(9:64)**

Once you leg is hooked and your inside wrist is captured in preparation for the Peterson Roll, you must react quickly to cup his head with your free hand. Pull his head toward you (9:63), lift your knee slightly, and scoot your knee over his head (9:64). 'Swim' your inside arm forward, and lock you hands trapping both his arms.

Crossbody/Double Crossbody

Mule Kick

(9:65)

(9:66)

The Mule Kick must be executed immediately after the Crossbody is applied. Straighten your leg as you kick it upward and backward (9:65, 9:66). Once your knee returns to the mat, move immediately to an offensive move.

Whip Down

(9:67)

Raise your outside knee with your foot remaining posted (9:67). Whip your knee downward hard as you duck your head and inside shoulder toward the mat. As he falls to his side, 'swim' your inside arm around his waist securing a reversal.

Hip Whip Crossover

(9:68)   **(9:69)**

Similar to the Whip Down, the Hip Whip Crossover also results in a reversal and perhaps nearfall points. As you raise your inside knee, reach back and grasp your opponent's hip (9:68). Jerk downward on the hip as you whip your raised knee toward the mat.(9:69) Push off your outside foot, keep your belly down, and cross over your opponent to secure a reversal

Five O'clock

(9:70)   **(9:71)**

(9:72)

(9:73)

Once the Crossbody is applied, immediately sit out to position your legs as the hands on the face of a clock at 5 o'clock (9:70). Reach under the opponent's leg with both your hands and raise it slightly (9:71). From this position there are two options available.

1. Post your inside hand, raise your hips, and rotate to your inside knee (9:72).

2. Throw his leg over your head as you scoot your hips away and turn on top of him (9:73).

Six O'clock

(9:74)

(9:75)

(9:76)

The Six O'clock technique involves force in two directions; directly forward and directly backward. Once the Crossbody is applied, immediately place your forehead on the mat for support. Reach around the inserted leg and lock your hands (9:74). Simultaneously jerk his leg toward 12 (directly forward) and kick you hooked leg directly toward six (9:75). Push off your outside foot, keep your belly down, and cross over your opponent (9:76) to secure a reversal.

Half Nelson

The Half Nelson is the mostly widely used technique for turning an opponent toward his back. On any level, you must be able to stop the half if you expect to win. Normally, Half Nelsons are executed with the opponent broken down flat on his stomach. However, some beginning or inexperienced wrestlers will try it with the defensive man still on his base.

Half Nelson from Your Knees

Wing Down

(9:77)

(9:78)

If an opponent applies a Half Nelson while you are still solidly on your base, the Wing Down is an effective technique. Grab his wrist securely and, raise your elbow (9:77). Clamp his elbow to your side as your drop your shoulder to the mat (9:78) Transfer your weight to your outside foot and hop over your opponent keeping your stomach toward the mat.

Half Nelson on Your Stomach

Look Away/Stop Sign

(9:79)   **(9:80)**

(9:81)   **(9:82)**

If the offensive man applies a Half Nelson while you are flat on your stomach, immediately grab his wrist, raise your head, and 'look away' from the pressure. Pull the hand down (9:79), grab it with two hands (9:80) and 'lock it out' by rotating your arm (9:81).

As you grab the wrist and raise your head, pull your outside knee forward (Stop Sign) to help prevent him from turning you (9:82).

Chickenwing / Double Chickenwing / Turkey Bar

(9:83)   **(9:84)**

(9:85)   **(9:86)**

(9:87)   **(9:88)**

Single Chickenwings and Turkey Bars are defended with the same technique. Whether on your knees or on your stomach, lock your hands (9:83), pull forward and whip your opponent to his side (9:84). Post your outside foot and hop over keeping your stomach toward the mat (9:85).

Double Chickenwings are thought by many wrestlers to be unstoppable, however, they are not. Once the opponent has secured both wings (9:86), immediately grab your stomach with both your hands and scoot your inside leg toward your opponent's legs (9:87).

As he starts to drive you over, pivot up on your bottom elbow and bottom leg, raise your upper body and turn him toward his back (9:88). Sit out and clamp your hands to your stomach to secure the reversal and possibly nearfall points or a pin.

3/4 Nelson

The 3/4 Nelson is a power move and most frequently used by those with long arms or excellent strength. There are three basic ways to defend against the 3/4 Nelson and each must be executed immediately before the offensive wrestler establishes too much leverage.

Watch TV

(9:89)

As a child lying in the floor watching TV, prop your chin on the heels of your hands with your elbows slightly spread (9:89).

Flatten Out

A second technique to prevent the ¾ Nelson is to simply 'flatten out' on your stomach and hold your head up. This makes it practically impossible to pull your head underneath your chest.

Hip-Over Cradle

(9:90)

A third technique to stop the 3/4 is the Hip-Over Cradle. Post your inside foot, raise your hips high into the air and immediately push off your outside foot toward your opponent (9:90). As he falls to his side, step over with the outside foot. Reach under his near leg and grab your leg. Reach around his head, release your thigh and lock your hands in a Cradle.

Headlever

Snatch to Switch

(9:91)

(9:92)

(9:93)

Once broken down to your stomach with your arm straight, immediately raise your hips by pushing off your top foot. Reach underneath your body and lock your hands (9:91). With your outside foot posted, push back hard into your opponent and jerk both hands up into the air (9:92). Pivot to your hip and switch (9:93) to complete a reversal.

Special Situation Defenses

Freeing an Ankle

Controlling ankles is an important part of breakdowns and rides. It is necessary to be able to free your ankles on the mat or when attempting to stand up.

On The Mat

(9:94)

(9:95)

As your ankle is grabbed, pivot toward the ankle as you raise your knee. Sit through to your hips as you grab his hand on your ankle (9:94). Your shoulder, knee, and foot should be in a straight line to prevent the top man from pulling it out to the side. Keeping your foot planted, back into your opponent to break his grip, and free your ankle. Sit out and turn in for an escape.(9:95)

Standing

(9:96)

As you begin to stand up, wrestlers frequently grab your outside ankle. Squat, grab his wrist (9:96), lock your arm straight, and stand up pulling his hand off your ankle to free it.

Freeing Arm Bars

(9:97) (9:98)

(9:99) (9:100)

(9:101) (9:102)

2 On 1

The key to freeing 'bars' is equalization of force or even possibly gaining an advantage, We've all seen wrestlers on the bottom struggle with a single bar controlling them. Use your other hand! Make it two versus two, plus your elbow and upper body power. Lock your hands, dig your elbows into the mat (9:97), straighten your arms as you push back into your opponent off your elbows (9:98). As your forearm is freed, secure a two-handed (9:99) grip on his wrist and lock it out by rotating your arm (9:100).

1 On 2

To defend the one on two (double bar) (9:101), post your elbows on the mat, back into the opponent and straighten your arms (9:102). Throw your hands backward forcing the offensive man to lose his grip. Secure control of one of his wrists and return to your base.

Getting Off your Back

Considered to be the worst position in wrestling to be in, it is possible to prevent a pin with proper technique. First, you must bridge high on the top of your head. As you drop toward the mat, rotate your hips and turn toward your stomach as you 'shoot' your arm between your stomach and your opponent's chest.

Five Musts for Defensive Competency

Always maintain a good stance.

Relax and be ready to react.

Punish your opponent physically when he goes underneath you.

Immediately turn your defense into an offense.

Remember that the best defense is always a great offense.

CHAPTER 10

Mat Strategy: Winning the Close Matches

A strategy is a plan of action to achieve a goal. Unfortunately for many excellent wrestlers, match strategy is rarely discussed by their coach. They always seem to lose the close matches by a supposedly, 'stupid mistake', usually within the final few seconds.

Following are seven typical situations where strategy can be the 'winner's edge'.

1. Control Hands

   Learn to control hands and be 'passively aggressive'. With only a few seconds remaining in a close match, learn to control hands and be 'passively aggressive'. Grabbing wrists, hands, and elbows prevents your opponent from gaining inside control or executing a move. Depending on the score, it is always okay to take a stalling warning, or a warning and a single penalty point rather than give up a takedown for two points in the final seconds of a match.

2. Avoid Scoring

   Realize there are times you should not try to score. Example: You are ahead by one (say, 7-6) with fifteen seconds remaining. There is absolutely no reason to attempt another tilt and risk getting rolled to your back or reversed. A three point win scores the same number of points (team or match) as a one point victory.

3. Stay Inbounds

   Know there are situations on the mat's edge where you do not want to go out of bounds to get a fresh start. If the top wrestler is really tough with tilts, turns, and pins, stay inbounds on the edge of the mat and let the clock run. If a turn, tilt, or pin is eminent, 'accidentally' sit, turn, crawl or roll out of bounds. Even if you are called for 'fleeing the mat', it is better than any of the alternatives listed.

4. False Starts

   You are 'gassed' and need a break. Two false starts are allowable without penalty—use them if you need them. On occasions, a false start can mean the difference in victory or defeat. Psychologically, the ten to fifteen second rest break while getting reset for a new start can be incredible. If on the bottom, the best time to false start is immediately after the top man places his hand on the elbow. If on the top, the best ways to false start are to place your hand on his elbow and immediately use your free hand to grab around his waist and pull him down or drop your weight on his back when kneeling to the top position.

As a coach, if I thought my wrestler need a 'breather', I would form a 'C' with my hand as a signal to false start. Remember: Two false starts are allowable, back-to-back if needed. It is not unsportsmanlike to wrestle within the rules.

5. Stay on Bottom

If an opponent is obviously superior 'on his feet', but chooses to ride instead, attempt reverses, but AVOID ESCAPING. Move around on the bottom keeping your head up, but refuse to allow him to return to his specialty by escaping.

6. Know the Time Remaining

Try to be conscious of the time remaining. Glance at the clock if you have a safe opportunity or focus on your coach's voice if he alerts you to a 'short time' remains. Many unnecessary points and match-deciding points are given up by releasing an opponent within the last five or ten seconds of a period.

7. Play the Edge

'Playing the edge' of the mat to avoid being taken down is a useful strategy under certain circumstances. Basically, when a wrestler 'plays the edge', he maneuvers away from the center of the mat enabling him to get out of bounds to avoid a takedown. To protect a lead, to prevent giving up a takedown, or to avoid contact, attempt outside sweep singles and swing toward the edge of the mat. Moving around in your stance (toward the edge of the mat), as if to 'set up' a move, may also be beneficial.

8. Put on your Running Shoes

By putting on your running shoes, I actually mean to AVOID CONTACT—run from him! With four or five seconds remaining and a two point lead, giving up a takedown is unexcusable. Move backward, move laterally, but avoid contact. Yes, you might get a warning, but that is much better than giving up a takedown.

The smart coach discusses mat strategy for all situations with his team. As the Boy Scout motto says, "Be prepared".

CHAPTER 11

Boredom and the Games Wrestlers Play

"All work and no play makes Jack a dull boy". This is a commonly quoted proverb meaning that without time off from intense work, a person becomes bored. I think we'll all agree that a bored wrestler is an unproductive wrestler. A small daily or weekly break from the grueling practice routine frequently reaps great results. History tells us that the sentiment expressed by this proverb was first recorded thousands of years ago by the Egyptian sage Ptahhotep, who wrote in 2400 B.C., "One that reckons accounts all the day passes not a happy moment. One that gladdens his heart all the day provides not for his house. The bowman hits the mark, as the steersman reaches land, by diversity of aim".

Though the hard-nosed, no nonsense coach thinks games and fun are a waste of good practice time, they actually reap great benefits throughout the season, especially near State time.

These games usually consist of short contests with simple rules, but can involve strength, balance, and quickness. Some competitions are intense enough to qualify as conditioning exercises, while others provide a few minutes of fun.

The Games Wrestlers Play

Hand to Hand Combat

Wrestlers stand facing each other, with right thumbs clasped, and feet flat on mat with the outside of their right feet touching. On the whistle, each tries to force the other to move his foot, release his grip or to fall to the mat.

Knee Sumo

Partners face each other on their knees with their hands in front. At signal, each attempts to knock the other over or out of the circle. They may move around, push, pull, or snap in attempts to get the opponent out of the circle or down on the mat.

Standing Sumo

Partners face each other standing with their hands in front. At signal, each attempts to knock the other out of the circle. They may move around, push, pull, or snap in attempts to get the opponent out of the circle or to touch the mat with something other than his feet.

Shoulder To Shoulder (From Standing or From the Knees)

The rules are the same as Sumo, except each wrestler keeps his hands locked behind his own back.

Over And Under (From Standing or From The Knees)

The rules are the same as Sumo, except each wrestler secures an 'over and under' position before the start.

Stork Battle

Wrestlers hold their left foot up with the left hand, while clasping his partner's right thumb. After ten hops, the coach blows the whistle and each wrestler jerks, pulls, pushes and hops around trying to make his partner fall down or release his foot.

Note: For variety, allow each to secure a grip on a tennis ball. Taking the tennis ball away from your partner also counts as a victory.

Knee Slap

Partners see how many times they can slap the other's knee without getting their knees slapped over a specific period of time (usually 30 seconds).

Knights on Horseback

With one wrestler on his hands and knees, the other sits on his back and locks his legs. The object is to knock all the other knights off their horses. Pulling of clothes and help from the horse is illegal. A knight is out if any part of his upper body touches the mat.

Hammerlock Competition

The bottom wrestler lies on his stomach with a tennis ball held underneath his chest with one hand. The top wrestler uses learned technique and leverage to pull the hand holding the tennis ball from underneath his opponent and places it on his back. The top man must secure possession of the tennis ball to win.

Hand Fighting for the Ball

On their feet and in a stance, each wrestler secures a tight grip on the tennis ball. On the coach's signal, each wrestler hand fights to secure possession of the tennis ball.

Pull Power

With wrestlers on their stomach, they grab the thumbs of their partner (opponent). Make sure the hands are above a taped strip (where the mat comes together). On the whistle, wrestlers use their arms, hands, wrists, shoulder, and elbows to pull the partner's waist across the tape strip. For variety, have one side roll to their right to get a new partner. The end wrestler, of course, goes to the other end. The match ups can be challenging and fun.

Four Man Pushup Contest

In groups of four, preferably near the same general size, wrestlers form a square as illustrated. Each wrestlers places his feet on the other wrestler's lower back, while have another wrestler's feet on his lower back. On the whistle, all wrestlers push up (at the same time) and hold the position as long as possible.

Frogs A' Leaping

Leap Frog/Drop Step Scoot

Facing each other at arm's length, one wrestler drop steps/scoots through his partner's legs. He stands up, turns, and leapfrogs over his partner (he has bent over to an elbow on knees position). This pattern is executed as many times as possible in thirty seconds.

Leap Frog Races

Wrestlers are divided into teams and standing in straight lines. The second wrestler leaps over the first, the third leaps over the first, second, etc. The patter continues until the last wrestler in line crosses the finish line. Note: Limit the number of steps a wrestler may take after leaping over the last wrestler bent over.

Leap Frog/Drop Step Scoot

This race is almost identical to the leap frog race, except the wrestlers, go over, under, over under, over, and under alternating the leap frog and drop step/scoot until they reach the end of the line.

Flag Fun

Using flags from physical education flag football, several fun competitions are possible in wrestling that develop quickness, agility, and the competitive edge.

Donkey Tails

The flags are tucked halfway into the wrestler's shorts creating a 'tail' effect. On the whistle, each wrestler attempts to grab his partner's flag. The Hi Crotch, Fireman's Carry, Snapdown, Sprawl, and Arm Drag are possible techniques to use to reach the partner's flag.

Sock Hop

The flag is tucked halfway into either of each wrestler's socks with the 'tail' on the outside

It's everybody for him self as each wrestler attempts to capture flags while protecting his own. Losing one's flag eliminates them from that competition only.

As a variation, the coach may decide to divide the wrestlers into red and green teams.

Relay Races

Relay races seem to always bring out the competitive nature and team spirit of wrestlers. Popular relay races include races from the following positions: bear crawl, GI Joe (army crawl), crab walk (forward and backwards), wheelbarrow, piggyback, seal walk (same as army except the ankles are crossed), and baby crawl (all fours). Medicine balls relays add excitement to the usually boring sprints.

Medicine Ball Mania

Medicine balls are great additions to wrestling conditioning activities and games.

Take Your Medicine (Ball)

In pairs, the wrestlers kneel and secure a firm arm lock around the medicine ball. On the whistle, each wrestler tries to take the ball from the other. Depending on the number of balls available, a quick tournament could be held in a reasonably short period of time. Pair the wrestlers in the competition as closely as possible in size. Also possible is a battle-back consolation tournament held simultaneously, perhaps by an assistant coach.

The Twist and Shout

Sitting behind each other in rows (feet to back), the wrestler must twist around (from the waist up) and hand the ball to the next man. He must turn in the opposite direction to pass it to the next wrestler. Each wrestler shout's "Win" as he hands-off the ball.

The Zoo Group

The wrestling games zoo has tigers, and snakes, and turtles (Oh, My!). It is permissible to change the names to that of your mascot if desired.

Tiger

After designating the area of play, three or four wrestlers are placed on their hands and knees become tigers. On the whistle, the tigers try to tag all the other wrestlers to eliminate them from competition. This continues until the final 3-4 remain. They become the tigers for the next round.

Snake

Snake is almost the same as tiger, except that when touched by a snake, you become one immediately. This game goes quickly and requires great agility and awareness to win.

Turtle

Turtle is very similar to Tiger and Snake, except a wrestler is only eliminated after the center turtles take him down (from their knees), and turn him onto his back.

CHAPTER 12

Designing a Practice Plan for Optimal Results

Practice plans are as varied as the coaches that make them. The daily practice routine depends primarily on the skill level and experience of team members, the coach's philosophy, the time in the season, the number of days before actual competition, and the team goals to be reached.

The typical workday practice may be divided into several, or all, of the following basic components:

Jumping Rope
Warm Up Drills
Takedown Drills
Takedown Defense
Breakdowns, Tilts, and Pinning Combinations
Breakdowns, Tilts, and Pinning Combinations Defense
Reversals and Escapes
Reversals and Escapes Defense
Standing Reversals and Escapes
Standing Reversals and Escapes Defense
Takedowns from Behind
Takedown Live Competition
Top-Bottom Live Competition
Conditioning Drills
Games

Though some areas require daily practice, some require only bi-weekly or weekly review, drill, and practice in competitive situations. Takedowns from behind and reversal/escapes from the standing position are often the most neglected area of technique. Drilling on both of these areas of technique twice a week will reap great benefits.

Warm Up Suggestions

Warm up exercises may include jogging, forward rolls, backward rolls, cartwheels, stretching exercises, or sport-specific drill. Examples of sport-specific wrestling warm up drills are; the Duckwalk, neck bridges, stance movement, drop steps, and shoulder rolls.

Jumping Rope

No wrestling practice warm up is complete without jumping rope. As a head coach for 30 years, less than ten of my wrestlers ever missed a single match due to a serious injury. Coaches have often questioned this statistic, but the facts are indisputable.

I attribute this incredibly low rate of serious injury to jumping rope. Jumping rope improves coordination, develops cardiovascular endurance, improves flexibility, and increases the body's core temperature. It is also a great exercise for last minute dehydration to 'make weight'.

Conditioning Exercises

Conditioning exercises are designed to push the wrestlers that 'extra mile' to develop endurance and mental toughness. I explain to wrestlers that, only after they are very tired can they begin to increase their endurance. "Everybody is tough when they are fresh", I explain to my team, "Champions are tough even when they are exhausted".

Often, beginning coaches think the only conditioning exercises available are pushups, sit ups, leg lifts, and sprints. Conditioning exercises, however, are almost unlimited in scope. My favorites are bear crawls, crab walks, leap frog, Indian runs, four-man pushups, and fun games.

Tapering Workouts

Tapering is important if wrestlers are to compete at their optimal level. Obviously, tapering is not necessary in the pre-competition phase of the season as you are trying to develop endurance.

Once competition has begun, a general 'rule of thumb' is to eliminate conditioning two days prior to the meet or tournament. The practice day prior to competition should consist of jumping rope, warm up drills, and getting down to weight. You want the wrestlers to be rested and eager for battle.

Toward the elimination series (district, regions, area, and state) tapering becomes very critical. Late in the season, wrestlers are often battered, bruised, and tired of the daily grind practice often offers. They need time to rest, recuperate, and recharge. Live wrestling should be carefully monitored and limited during the weeks of elimination series competition. Without making them paranoid, instruct wrestlers to be extra careful in potentially dangerous situations and release the partner to avoid injury.

A season-ending injury in practice with only a few weeks left, is 'un-excusable', at best.

Believe it or not, Ripley!

While serving as the host coach for the 1988 Georgia AAA State tournament, I received a call on the Thursday night before competition was to begin Friday morning. The coach reported that his top-seeded wrestler had broken his ankle and needed to be 'scratched from the tournament'. When I inquired as to how the injury occurred, he responded, "He was running up the stadium steps this afternoon to get into shape, slipped on the ice, and fell." UNBELIEVABLE! I thought, "How much can you improve your conditioning in the last day before State?" Use common sense with conditioning, realize most athletes are already 'in shape' by the end of the season, and taper appropriately for the final battles.

CHAPTER 13

Safety in the Practice Room

10 Rules That Must Not Be Ignored

With the current focus on legal liability, and the increasing number of lawsuits that are filed against school systems, safety in the practice room is of utmost importance. Suggestions to avoid injuries and maintain a safe environment for practice include:

1. Keep the room clean.

    Daily sweeping and spraying, or mopping of the mats is imperative. There are several products on the market that will destroy potentially hazard viruses and bacteria. Some coaches delegate the responsibility to wrestlers and post a weekly schedule.

2. Make sure edges and corners are all well-padded.

3. Provide a means for wrestlers to wipe their feet.

    There should always be a method by which everyone that enters the practice area can wipe their feet. Today's market has several trays that can be filled with cleaning solutions and placed at the room's entrance. The entire area, not only the mats, should remain clean.

    Wrestlers should never wear their shoes out of the wrestling room (area) or outdoors.

4. Provide a container for trash. A small garbage can in which all waste can be deposited including first aid materials. Require proper disposal of all hazardous materials (blood and body-fluids)

5. Keep a completely stocked first aid kit in the room.

    Head Trainers are usually more than willing to provide a stocked first aid kit for the student trainers or coaches to use in the practice room and also to carry to competitions.(Never assume trainers will be available at away competitions.) Basic requirements are : nose plugs, band aids, gauze pads, tape, scissors, pre-wrap, antibacterial spray, elastic wraps, ice, contact lens solution and holder, and hand wipes or cleaner.

6. Always have phone access.

   With the popularity of cell phones, this requirement is easily met. Not only is it necessary for 911 calls, it is important to notify parents in the event of any major injuries.

7. Competitors should be grouped according to weight.

   It is illegal, illogical and absolutely unreasonable to group wrestlers for practice if they have extreme weight differences. It would be hard to justify in court why a 160# wrestler was allowed to practice with and seriously injure a 130# teammate.

8. Competitors should be grouped according to ability and experience when competing.

   While it is often beneficial to have an experienced athlete work with a new or basically inexperienced one, never allow a stud to just beat down a new guy. Group the studs and occasionally mix them in with the newer guys so they can get the feel of wrestling tough competition.

9. Never permit wrestlers with infectious skin diseases to participate in practice.

   Although we want every guy to practice every day, sometimes we have to do what's best for the kid and the team. The risk of spreading the problem (herpes, ringworm, impetigo) to the team is not worth the risk. Covering the infection DOES NOT prevent it from spreading.

10. Never allow an injured wrestler to practice.

   This rule doesn't apply to those with minor scrapes, bruises, and strains who have been seen and released by the trainer. For your protection and that of the athlete, NEVER ignore a doctor or trainer's requirements or suggestions regarding an athlete's participation in practice or competitions.

CHAPTER 14

Setting SMARTER Goals

Goal setting plays an important role in almost every aspect of our lives. We've all had homeroom teachers or counselors in high school and college that directed us through the process of setting short, intermediate, and long range goals. Most were concerned with the educational aspects of our lives, but often included goals related to the financial, social, and personal (moral, religious, physical condition) areas. These goals were intended to motivate us to higher levels of performance and provide us with direction. The old story about a person without goals being like 'a ship without a sail', is still true today, especially in the sports arena. The athlete who 'sails' through his career with no defined direction or destination is doomed to sink (fail).

Goals are motivational tools that provide us with focus, direction, and a means of evaluating performance. For wrestlers competing in the achievement-based arena of sport, goal setting is imperative. Attempting to wrestle without definite goals would be a, as the beautiful Julia Roberts said, "Big mistake. Big. Huge."

Much has been written about the guidelines and principles of goal setting in athletics. The best information available also seems to be the SMARTEST information available. This catchy acronym provides comprehensive guidance in the goal setting process.

S Specific
Goals should be as specific as possible. "To get better" is an admirable goal, but difficult to measure. More specific goals would be "To win 75% of all my matches this season", "To place in every tournament", "To win the state championship". These are all examples of specific goals that leave no doubt as to the outcome desired.

M Measurable
Success in attaining your desired goals must be measurable. A common example of a measurable goal would be, "To drop to the 103# weight class before Districts." Weight loss is easily measured and a common goal for wrestlers. Charting progress is simple, provides immediate feedback, and provides motivation that will help guide you toward your goal.

A Attainable
Unrealistic and unattainable goals are a waste of one's time and counter-productive to success. Inappropriate goals often lead to unnecessary anxiety, stress, and ultimately, failure. Challenging goals that are attainable with hard work, dedication, sacrifice, and 'a little luck' are ideal. Remember though, "The harder you work, the luckier you get".

R Recorded

Simply put, goals should be written down. Some athletes post them on their locker, on the refrigerator (especially weight loss), or on the mirror at home. The list is a way of making a formal contract with your self to work hard to attain each goal specified.

T Time-specific

Set specific time limits for attaining your goals. Whether short, medium, or long range, goals should have a definite time frame for achievement. "To earn a college wrestling scholarship by the end of my senior season" or "To attend two camps this summer" are time-specific goals. Short-term goals are considered the most important because they provide focus and inspiration for daily workouts and dieting regiments.

E Evaluate

Your progress should be evaluated on a regular basis. With goals that are specific, recorded, and measurable, progress (or the lack of it) is easily identified. If your progress is lacking, adjust your workouts, attitude, effort or commitment. If you reach a goal quicker than expected, establish a new goal that will motivate you to achieve even greater success.

R Revisable

Under certain circumstances, it may become necessary to revise one's goals. In instances of prolonged illness, injury, or other unexpected roadblocks, revise or reset your goals to reflect realistic expectations.

Examples of SMARTER goals include:

Short Term

Attend all scheduled practices and weight training sessions.
Learn and drill on two new takedowns.
Jump rope for fifteen consecutive minutes on three days
Run one mile after practice two days per week.
Be 'on time' for all wrestling functions.

Intermediate Term

Win 80% of my dual matches this season.
'Make weight' for all the meets and tournaments.
Place in the top four of all regular season invitational tournaments.
Win the Texas State Championship.
Attend 75% of the in-state freestyle and Greco-Roman tournaments.

Long Term

Attend college on a wrestling scholarship.
Place in the USA Junior Nationals tournament.
Wrestle in the Olympics
Earn a college degree and secure a job as a high school wrestling coach.

Ultimately, each wrestler is responsible for setting his own individual goals. The coach, and even the parents, may help guide the athlete providing input and direction, but in the final analysis, the individual is the one person responsible for his own decisions. He is the one who will be required to attend the workouts, run the sprints, jump the rope, wrestle the matches, make the weight, and push himself toward success.

Remember, as one of my old t-shirts once proclaimed, "Happy are those who dream dreams and pay the price to make them come true". Dream your dreams, set your goals, pay the price, and they will come true.

CHAPTER 15

Ten Exercises For Developing Strong Wrestlers

"Only the strong survive" is a phrase which is shorthand for a concept relating to competition for survival or predominance. In wrestling, it simply means that with skill being equal, the strongest will usually win.

Strength training regiments are as numerous and varied as the coaches that develop them.

Through forty-five years of wrestling and coaching wrestlers, I have found ten exercises that will develop total body strength. Weight amounts and repetitions are determined by the individual coach and his objectives.

Although the exercises strengthen the total body, close examination will reveal there is a focus on arm, chest, and grip strength due to the nature of the sport.

1. Rocky Sit ups

   Cover the squat bar with a thick towel or pad. Hang by your knees and complete sit ups as Rocky did in his training routine. As you sit up, touch your elbows to the opposing knees.

2. "Good Morning"

   'Good Morning', commonly known as Backups, got its' name from the bowing motion as if greeting another person. With the legs secured and hips on the bar, place both hands behind your head and bend over at the waist until perpendicular to the floor. Arch up. Hold the position for a second, relax, and repeat the exercise as instructed.

3. Overload Dips

   Overload dips require three chairs (or benches) and selected weight plates. From a sitting position, place one hand in each chair and your feet in the other. Keep your legs straight and hips at ninety degrees. After your partner places the weight plate on your thighs, complete the dips as instructed.

4. Overload Pushups

From a normal pushup position, your partner places the appropriate weight plate between your shoulder blades. Keeping your head up, lower your chest until it touches the floor and push up.

Repeat as directed by the workout plan.

5. Lunges

Holding selected weight plate, step forward and drop your back knee to the floor. Step up and repeat the process using the other leg. Continue the procedure across the room or assigned distance.

6. Neck Series

With one wrestler on his base, the partner kneels directly in front of him. Using the open hand, push against the side of the bottom man's head as he moves it laterally. Change sides of the head and repeat. Next, using both hands, push down on the top of his head as he raises it. Change hand position to pull up on his chin as he pulls his chin to his chest. Repeat as directed.

7. Grippers

Grippers are, as the name implies, designed to improve grip strength. Research has shown a positive correlation between grip strength and wrestling success. Select a weight plate, place a hand on your knee for support, and step the opposite foot back for safety. Raise the weight slightly, release it, and catch it on the way down. Continuing the motion, repeat the exercise for the desired number of repetitions.

8. Popeye Roll Ups

Popeye Roll Ups (named after the cartoon characters forearms) require a dowel (12:18"), a piece of rope, and a weight plate. Tie the rope to the plate and then to the dowel. Stand on a chair (if required or desired), extend your arms and lock the elbows. Using only the wrists and forearms, roll the weight up and slowly roll it back down. Allowing the rope to unroll quickly conflicts with the desired objective and must be avoided.

9. Bench Pulls

Lying face-down on a bench, grip the weighted bar at a shoulder—width distance. Pull the bar up until it touches the bench, relax, lower the weight to the floor and repeat as directed.

10. Triple Threat

The Triple Threat is a total shoulder girdle workout. It consists of consecutive sets of upright rowing, curls, and reverse curl repetitions. Numbers of repetitions and sets are determined by the coach.

CHAPTER 16

Mental Skills: The Competitive Edge

"Baseball is 90% mental, the other half is physical." according to the former New York Yankee great, Yogi Berra. While many of us might question Yogi's math prowess, few would question his belief that the mental aspect of athletics plays a big role in one's success.

Mental preparation in athletic competition has been around for centuries. Athletes of ancient times realized they had to 'get their mind right' before they performed. Many of these 'ancient warriors' meditated before competitions.

Seemingly, coaches always knew that somehow, the mental aspect of sports was important. The extent of mental skills implementation by coaches in past decades was a simple, "Keep your head in the game" or "Relax and hit the ball" or "You can if you think you can" word of encouragement.

Even today, the importance of mental skills is often neglected by coaches and, as a result, many of their wrestlers never reach their full potential. Recent scientific studies (over the last couple of decades), have consistently shown that mental skills training will improve the athlete's psychological skills, and ultimately it increase his athletic performance.

As three-time NCAA Champion, Mark Churella observed, "It's the mental aspect of wrestling that takes first place at the (NCAA) tournament and the physical aspect of it takes second place. Everyone comes in physically prepared. It's how well they mentally prepare that makes the difference."

My former assistant, the late Beasey Hendrix, was a pioneer in formal mental skills training techniques. He often commented that several 'old school' coaches referred to mental skills training as voodoo, black magic, or trickery. "The fear of the unknown has been around for ages", Beasey said, "but the wise coaches learn about the 'unknown' and use it to their benefit".

Our mental skills program at Troup High School (GA) was comprised of simulation, focus and concentration, positive self-talk, visualization, stress reduction through relaxation, and developing strategies in preparing for competition.

Stress—The Champion Killer

Stress, and the wrestlers' inability to deal with it, has put many skilled athletes in the bleachers when they should have been standing on the podium. Stress can be beneficial to an extent in preparing for a match, but also be the champion-killer (enemy) if left unmanaged.

First, we need to realize that stress affects wrestlers in different ways. Some sense a form of nervousness in their body and feel 'uptight', 'tense', or even 'frozen'. Others may sense the 'negative talk' in their head. "He's so big and muscled-up". "My back is hurting.", I'll never take him down". "I can't beat a Region champion."

Either of these types, physical or mental, can negatively affect one's performance on the mat. Each can dominate the mind and shift focus from the task at hand (the match) to the psychological issues (real or imagined) floating through one's head.

Through research, methods have been developed to deal with, reduce, eliminate, or at least learn to control both types of stress.

Somatic stress, also known as body stress, is the process of reacting physically to a situation. Your body becomes very tense. The following diagram shows the vicious circle created by anxiety (nervousness), bodily stress, and poor performance.

ANXIETY

↑   ↓

BODILY STRESS   ←   POOR PERFORMANCE

Cognitive stress, (negative thinking), causes the wrestler to build anxiety by thinking negatively about an upcoming event or task. These thoughts then cause physical symptoms that may interfere with the wrestler's performance. The objective is to stop the negative thoughts and progress to positive thinking. Sounds easy, but it can often be difficult to train yourself to stop and refocus. The following diagram shows the cycle created by negative thinking.

NEGATIVE THINKING

↑   ↓

BODILY STRESS   ←   PERFORMANCE PROBLEMS

The Art of Relaxation

Relaxation is a technique that enables the wrestler to relax his body, remove stress, and clear the mind to enable positive thinking. Relaxation is based primarily upon clearing one's mind and calming one's body. Progressive relaxation seems to be the most readily accepted and widely used method among wrestlers.

Make An Arrest!

The most common method of arresting physical tension development is deep breathing exercises. First, find a quiet place, loosen clothing, take your shoes off (or at least loosen your shoestrings), and lie down.

You must then search (scan) your body for relaxed areas. Focus on theses areas and remain calm. Think back to a time when you were very, very tired. Mentally capture this feeling. Focus on that feeling and think about the physical sensations. Close your eyes. Think about the 'tired moment', take a deep breath, and slowly blow it out. Take another slow deep breath. As you blow it out, imagine a long stream of tension and stress leaving your body. Your body will settle into a nice, heavy, relaxed, and comfortable position.

Next, focus on your legs. Tell them to relax and allow them to feel very heavy. Now, repeat the procedure with your arms, hands, back, and neck.

Smile to yourself mentally and think of a nice, relaxing time in your life. Some wrestlers like to think of an air mattress floating in a swimming pool. Others like thinking of lying on a sofa as most relaxing. Personally, thinking of lying on a breezy beach with the ocean waves lapping my feet, always put me in the 'zone'. Regardless, think of a situation where you were completely in control and totally comfortable.

Focus on that feeling of calmness, empty your mind of 'thought' words and replace them with 'feeling words'. "Relax, calm, peaceful, light, happy, relax, happy, peaceful, and calm", you should repeat to yourself. Focus on these feelings.

Find the heaviest, most relaxed part of your body and ask that feeling to spread across your body. You should begin to feel heavier and heavier. You should now be completely relaxed and calm. Kick back and enjoy this feeling.

Focus only on the positive, stay in your zone, and have a great time making the 'arrest'.

Training via Simulation

Simulation training attempts to duplicate the conditions one can expect in the competitive environment. Smart coaches manipulate the practice environment to create all possible stresses under which his athletes may have to perform.

These simulation activities seek to train the total body to perform under duress and distractions. Having trained under the conditions previously, the wrestler will be able to relax and feel as if he has 'been there before' and it's no big deal.

Possible Stresses to be Introduced by the Coach

1. Practice on Saturday mornings starting at 9:00 or 10:00. These practices simulate a tournament's semi-final round in most cases and athletes' bodies must be able to perform.

2. Train at different room temperatures. Turn the thermostat down to 68 degrees or turn it up to 90. Not all competition facilities keep the temperature at 72.

3. Train immediately after a big meal. Several wrestlers, possibly all, mistakenly overeat after weigh-in and can't 'deal with it'. Having trained on a 'full stomach' is an added advantage.

4. Have all wrestlers fast the entire day before the evening workout. This is a common practice among regular 'weight-cutters', but almost all wrestlers will face this situation during their career. Wrestlers will learn to 'pace themselves, conserve energy, and focus on executing perfect technique to secure a victory.

5. Have simulated duels (intra-squad) including an official, relaxation sessions, pre-match rituals. Have the official make a few 'bad calls' to see how certain individuals react.

6. Make practice tougher than any match could possibly be.

Wrestling under these tough conditions will reap many rewards. Athletes will gain confidence that they can 'handle anything' as they have 'been there before'. They will develop confidence in their ability to maintain a high level of skill under any condition.

As Louis Pasteur said, "Chance favors the prepared mind". Had Louis been a wrestling coach, his quote would have probably said, "Chance favors the prepared mind and the prepared body."

Positive Self-Talk—"I Think I Can, I Think I Can"

The Little Engine That Could, is a moralistic children's story used to teach children the value of optimism and hard work. In the tale, a long train must be pulled over a high mountain. Various larger engines, treated anthropomorphically, are asked to pull the train; for various reasons they refuse. The request is sent to a small engine, who agrees to try. The engine succeeds in pulling the train over the mountain while repeating its motto: "I-think-I-can".

This is an excellent example of an affirmation, or a statement that gives one self confidence and allows the person to believe in himself. Affirmations are now used by world-class athletes and are a necessity for optimal success on a high school level.

The following is a list of common affirmations we used at Troup High School (GA). Review the list and select the ones you would like to incorporate into your pre-match ritual or match dialogue.

Wrestlers may feel awkward at first, but can train themselves to believe by constantly repeating the statements.

Sample Affirmations
I am best prepared.
I am tougher.
I want it more.
I will stay focused.
My endurance is awesome.
I will break him mentally.
I am in great shape.
I will win.
I am better coached.
I am unbeatable.
I am the man.
He can't turn me.
No one holds me down.
I am an animal on top.
I've had great workouts.
I made weight right.
I got plenty of rest.
Nobody takes me down.
I am ready for greatness.
I believe in myself.
I feel strong.
I refuse to lose.
I am ready.
And as the little engine said, "I think I can".

Focusing

Focus is defined as the ability to concentrate on a specific idea or area of thought. It allows us to function successfully in a complicated environment while our senses constantly receive varied data. Without the ability to focus, we would be overloaded and unable to function properly, especially in the wrestling arena.

Problems arise in wrestling when the athlete focuses on things that are not important or fails to focus on the important ideas regarding the situation at hand. Focusing on negatives is counter-productive to success and should be avoided. Negative focus 'freezes' us and keeps our attention glued to the problem at hand. This negative focus leaves little room for clear thinking regarding corrections or improvements.

When your mind begins to wander to negative issues, simply use the following game plan to redirect negative thinking:

1. Realize it.

2. Stop it!

3. Redirect your thoughts.

Visualization

Visualization is another advantageous technique. In visualization, the athlete sees what he wants to do. He mentally pictures himself being successful in executing moves, winning matches, and standing on the podium. Visualization is instrumental in developing confidence and competency.

Kendall Cross, a 1996 Olympic gold medalist, explained how he sees visualization working for him. "Your mind has trouble distinguishing between actual physical motion and mental imagery of that same motion. To the mind it is all the same. Therefore, it is effective to visualize yourself performing perfect techniques. It gives your mind a blueprint for those techniques. Granted you must practice them physically as well to develop the motor skills for that movement. Visualization is great because you can practice that art anytime. Before the 1996 Olympic Trials, I used visualization every chance I could find. I used it at home while listening to my favorite music, while riding a stationary bike, sitting on an airplane, riding in a car, and just about any other time I could free my mind of distraction."

"My visualization was multi-faceted. Not only did I visualize perfect technique, but I also saw the arena, the crowd, the referee, ... everything that goes along with the actual match". I would try to smell the gym, my opponent, popcorn at the concession stand, etc. The idea was to try to recruit my other senses to make it feel as real as possible".

Help your wrestlers develop a visualization ritual and it will pay great benefits. As the old saying goes, "To be it, you must first see it."

Preparing For Competition

The following list of suggestions was developed to aid in preparing for wrestling competition. For athletes who feel as though they are doing well with their present routine, great! For those who need help, these guidelines may be beneficial:

1. Become self-centered. Listen to music and stay alone.

2. Plan your attack. Develop your 'plan of action'.

3. Have a plan for unexpected developments (bad calls, getting thrown to your back, etc.)

4. Pace your warmup to reach optimum readiness just before your match.

5. Focus on the task at hand. Block out all distractions.

6. Rid your mind of any negative self-talk.

7. Hit your 'zone', mentally.

8. Step on the mat and PERFORM!

"In a wrestler's preparation, mental-skills training is as important as any technical or physical training. For the total package, one needs to be strong in all areas of wrestling. When the technical, physical, and psychological come together as one, now you are on to something", according to Steve Fraser, an Olympic gold medalist for the United States.

CHAPTER 17

Weight Management for Wrestlers

Drastic weight loss procedures and associated deaths have brought more negative publicity and attention to our sport than any issue in the history of amateur wrestling. If any 'good' came from the 'bad', it would have to be the constant focus on healthy and safe weight management practices and the passing of legislation by the state athletic associations to insure enforcement of these practices.

Today, each state is responsible for establishing and enforcing its own weight certification procedures, weight loss guidelines, and weigh-in procedures. The wise coach will strictly adhere to his state association's weight-related policies to protect him from potential litigation and also to insure optimum performance by his wrestlers.

Research has shown that practicing proper methods of weight control is necessary for optimal performance by wrestlers. Peak performance can only occur when the body is adequately supplied with an appropriate amount of the essential nutrients. Using improper methods of weight control including fasting, dehydration, yo-yo dieting, and diet pills, will decrease your level of performance. The Wrestler's Diet (provided by the California Interscholastic Federation) provides the necessary information to help you achieve the highest level of performance possible. The psychological advantages of maintaining good nutritional practices are great: you'll wrestle better if you feel good physically and mentally. You will also wrestle better knowing that you have done everything possible to be at your best.

Sample Menus and Snacks: 2,000 Calories

Breakfast

Blender Drink

Banana, 1 100
Milk, 1 cup 2% 120
Peanut Butter, 1t 95
Jam, 1t 15
Calories.. 400

Lunch

Hamburger on Bun
Bun 120
Grnd. Beef, 2 oz 120
Catsup, 1T 20
French Fries..220
Milk, 1 cup 2% 120
Oatmeal Raisin Cookies(2)
(2 1/2" diameter)...............................120
Calories.................................... 760

Dinner

Roast Pork, 3 oz 220
Baked Potato 100
Broccoli, 1 stalk...................................20
Margarine, 2t 70
Bread, 1 slice 70
Sliced peaches, 1 cup...........................130
Milk, 1 cup 2% 120
Calories.................................... 730

Snack
Lo-cal Pudding, 1 cup 130
Total Calories................................ 2020

Breakfast

Grapefruit Juice, 6 oz 75
Unsweetened Cereal,1 cup 110
Banana, 1 medium 100
Milk, 1 cup 2% 120
Toast, 1 slice..70
Margarine, 1t 35
Jam, 1t 15
Calories...................................... 525

Lunch

Chicken Salad Sandwich
Bread, 2 slices.....................................140
Chicken Breast, 2 oz...........................120

Lo Cal Dressing, 1T 30
Milk, 1 cup 2%....................................120
Apple, 1 medium 80
Calories................................... **490**

Dinner

Chili, 2 cups...600
Saltine Crackers, 12...............................160
Milk, 1 cup 2% 120
Carrot and Celery Sticks.........................10
Calories................................... **890**

Snack
Orange, 1 medium 80
Total Calories.................................. **2025**

Breakfast

Apple Juice, 6 oz....................................90
Oatmeal, 1 cup.....................................145
Raisins, 1T 30
Milk, 1 cup 2% 120
Toast, 1 slice..70
Margarine..35
Calories 490

Lunch

"Sloppy Joe"
Hamburger Filling, 2 oz 200
Bun 140
Carrot and Celery Sticks.........................10
Milk, 1 cup 2% 120

Chocolate Chip Cookie
1 small...50
Calories... **520**

Dinner

Turkey Tacos
Taco Shells, 3 210
Picante Sauce, 2 oz 30

American Cheese,
4 oz. shredded 220
Ground Turkey, 4 oz.............................310

Lettuce, Onion, Tomato, etc10
Milk, 1 cup 2% 120
Calories.............................. 900

Snack
Orange, 1 medium 80
Total Calories............................. 1990

Breakfast

Orange Juice 6 oz 80
English Muffin.....................................140
Peanut Butter, 1T.................................90
Banana, 1 medium 100
Milk, 1 cup 2% 120
Calories............................... 530

Lunch

Cheese Pizza, 2 slices 400
Milk, 1 cup 2% 120
Apple, 1 medium 80
Calories............................... 600

Dinner

Chicken and Noodles,
1 cup...300
Cooked Carrots, 1/2 cup 25
Lettuce Salad 10
Dressing, 1T 60
Milk, 1 cup 2% 120
Calories............................... 515

Snack

Milk, 1 cup 2% 120
Fig Bars, 5 250
Calories 370
Total Calories 2015

Breakfast

French Toast,

2 slices 300
Syrup, 2 oz 200
Strawberries, 4 oz.(unsweetened 25
Milk, 1 cup 2% 120
Calories 645

Lunch

Turkey Sandwich

Bread, 2 slices 140
Turkey Breast, 3 oz 105
Lettuce, Tomato Slices 5
Lo-cal Mayonnaise, 1T 30
Milk, 1 cup 2% 120
Calories 400

Dinner

Beef Stew, 2 cups 400
Dinner Roll, 1 70
Margarine, 1t 35
Applesauce, 4 oz 55
Milk, 1 cup 2% 120
Lo-cal Pudding, 1 cup 130
Vanilla Wafers, 6 100
Calories 910

Snack

Popcorn, 2 cups, no butter 60
Diet Soda, 12 oz 0
Calories 60
Total Calories 2015

Breakfast

Cantaloupe, 1/4 60
Egg, poached 75
Toast, 2 slices 140
Margarine, 1t 35
Jam, 2t 30
Milk, 1 cup 2% 120
Calories 460

Lunch

Tuna Pocket
Pita Bread, 1 120
Tuna, 3 oz 100
Lo-cal Mayonnaise, 2T 60
Lettuce, tomato slices 5
Pretzels, 1 oz 110
Milk, 1 cup 2% 120
Calories 515

Dinner

Broiled Turkey Breast, 3 oz 130
Wild Rice Pilaf, 1 cup 270
Spinach Salad 15
Dressing, 1T 60
Angel Food Cake, 1 slice 125
Chocolate Syrup, 2T 75
Milk, 1 cup 2% 120
Calories 795

Snack
Pineapple, 1 cup 150
Graham Crackers, 3 squares 80
Calories 23
Total Calories 2000

CHAPTER 18

Teaching Technique: The DANIEL Method

Teaching technique is a primary responsibility of wrestling coaches. By teaching, I mean the successful transfer of knowledge from the coach to the athletes on his team.

The first step in successful transfer is providing an environment conducive to learning. The wrestlers must be SILENT to LISTEN. Interestingly, they are both spelled with the same letters.

Secondly, wrestlers need to determine their dominant learning style. They learn best with a particular style, but need to use all three when possible.

Auditory learners must hear the name of the technique and the key words that describe the action. Silence enables these learners to focus on the voice of the presenter.

Visual learners must be able to have an unobstructed view of the technique. Visual learners like to see things and can actually get a better idea of what to do by watching the demonstration carefully.

Tactile learners must be able to physically practice the move. Although everyone must drill on the move, tactile learners really like to feel the pressures and the movements. They should be used as demonstration partners whenever possible to enhance their learning.

Teaching a move involves more than just showing a move and telling the guys to 'drill on it". Over the past forty years I develop a successful strategy for teaching technique. Appropriately, I call it the DANIEL Method. Each letter represents a step in my teaching of technique that has proven over the years to produce winners.

D Demonstrate

Demonstrate the technique to the entire team or group. For wrestling, the whole-part-whole method seems to be best. The whole skill is first demonstrated before being broken down into the constituent parts to practice the individual elements and improve on these, before putting the whole skill back together. This can be very effective in skills which have easily distinguished parts, where the whole skill together is complex. A good example in wrestling is where the athlete would practice the whole move then isolate a weak component, such as the hip pivot in a Switch, before putting the whole move back together. This gives the athlete a sense of the whole skill before they break it down and improve on the weak aspects of the performance.

A Analyze

Analyze the move thoroughly. Point out the pressure points, the leverages, the forces, the torque, and the power used in various phases of the move. It is beneficial when you have finished demonstrating a move, to have your wrestlers 'talk you through it', step by step, to assure they know it thoroughly.

N Name

Name the move. Although books have been written on wrestling nomenclature in an effort to standardize terminology, it is a losing effort. There are still several names for the same technique in different states or areas of the country.

Decide the one you like best and stick with it. It will develop consistency in your total program and help tremendously in yelling instructions during a match. 'Catchy' names seem to be more fun for kids and definitely easier to remember. Some of my favorites are the Roach Motel, Ripper, Snake, and the Saturday Night Ride.

I Insist

Insist on focus and perfect technique when drilling. Though it is unrealistic to expect perfect technique immediately, insist that your wrestlers work toward that goal. To permit poor technique in drills is to promote poor technique in drills.

E Encourage

Encourage your wrestlers by praising them for performing the skill, or any part of it, correctly. Immediate praise works best. Praise may only be a simple, "Good job", Nice setup", "Great technique", or "Good job on following through". When correcting a part of the move, always begin the correction with a positive statement. This prevents the athlete from instantly becoming defensive and tuning you out. An example would be, "You had a great stance and took him down, but you need to lower your level for more power". Regardless of how poor the move was overall, you can always fine a positive part of the effort to reinforce.

L Let 'em

Let 'em drill, and drill, and then . . . . drill some more. Repetitions of proper technique develop muscle memory, endurance, confidence, and eventually . . . . CHAMPIONS.

Don't Say Don't

If I could make only one suggestion to coaches regarding the teaching of technique, it would be, "Don't say don't". I have always been amused by coaches who spend most of their demonstration time telling athletes what NOT to do. I believe wrestlers would never think of doing the things coaches tell them not to do if the coach didn't mention it first.

Tell them where to put their hands, where to put their feet, where to place their head, which direction to push, and which direction to turn. These are the type of instructions athletes need to hear. Rather than waste your time with the 'do not', tell them the 'do'. You'll be amazed at the difference it makes.

Rather than say, "Don't let him up to his base", say "Keep him flat on his stomach".

Rather than say, "Don't reach over his shoulder", say "Reach under his arm".

Rather than say, "Don't let him control your wrists", say "Keep your wrists free".

Rather than say, "Don't let him go out of bounds", say "Keep him in bounds".

Rather than say, "Don't cross your feet", say "Keep your feet apart".

Rather than say, "Don't look toward the Half ", say "Look away from the Half".

CHAPTER 19

The Administration of Competition

Hosting competitions can very challenging, but also rewarding and satisfying. Well-planned and properly administered competitions can be financially beneficial with profits in the thousands possible. In addition, the reputation of the team, athletic department, school and community can be enhanced with completion of a successful event.

Excellent tournaments and dual meets don't 'just happen' they are the result of careful planning and organization. The following guidelines regarding the administration of competition have been developed through the hosting of hundreds of dual meets and scores of tournaments on the local, state, and national level.

Remember: People don't PLAN to FAIL, they just FAIL to PLAN.

The first phase of hosting a tournament consists of planning the administrative details.

Set a date. Try to select a date that does not conflict with an established tournament in your area.

Decide the level and format of competition. Will it be middle school, junior varsity, varsity, or a combination? Will it be a team dual, individual pool, or regular double-elimination format?

Decide the host location. It may be your school, your middle school, or a city auditorium. Make sure the facility is available and get the agreement in writing.

Set an entry fee. Some districts limit the amount of entry fee that can be charged, but usually you determine what the 'market can bear'. Try to stay consistent with the fees other tournaments in your area charge. With strictly individual tournaments with no team scoring, tournaments usually charge a school 'per entry' or 'team' prices like $10 per entry or $150 per team. This allows team with large numbers to participate without draining their budget. It also gets greater numbers to the concession stand so you don't actually 'lose money'.

Name the tournament. Try to be creative and attention-getting. Make it something you wish to be identified with for a long time. Our Allen (TX) middle school level tournament is the A-TOWN SHOWDOWN Middle School Invitational. Coppell (TX) hosts a holiday tournament called the 'SANTA SLAM'. South Grand Prairie (TX) hosts the LONE STAR DUALS.

Select a Tournament Director. This person should be selected for his organizational and public relations skills. He should be able to delegate responsibility, communicate well, and have the patience of Job. Simply speaking, he is the 'go to' person when questions or problems arise.

Recruit participant schools. Design a flyer and distribute it to coaches at pre-season scheduling meeting. Post the event on available forums, mail invitations, call coaches, get the word out! Be careful to stay within the number of entrants your facility or time restraints can adequately handle.

Send information regarding local motel numbers and rates, as well as local restaurant information, to out-of-town teams requiring overnight accommodations.

Develop committees and appoint chairmen. At a preseason Takedown Club or Booster Club meeting, recruit volunteers for the following various committees required for success.

Committees needed include:

Hospitality Room

The hospitality room is an important part of every tournament. The primary responsibility of the hospitality committee is to provide food for the guests and to make them feel welcomed. A carefully planned schedule of appropriate foods is a necessity to leave a good impression. With normal community support, much of the food in the hospitality room is donated. Many moms are very creative in designing table centerpieces with wrestling themes.

As an added touch, place a few of your team's season programs on the tables

The personnel in charge should be aware of times the breaks in action are scheduled to prepare for the 'rush'. The coaches, officials, tournament personnel, and the media are usually the only persons admitted to the hospitality room. Tournaments with large numbers may use color-coded wrist bands to control access to the area. For best results, refreshments should be available immediately as the people arrive on site. Note: If there is a seeding meeting on a day prior to the tournament, soft drinks, water, and snacks should be provided there also.

Awards

After the approximate number of entries has been finalized, awards should be ordered. Awards are typically presented to individuals who place 1st-4th or 1st-6th, depending on entries, finances, and preference. Individual awards vary in price from .99 up to $4.00 or more depending on style, size, and quantities ordered. Traditionally, team trophies or plaques are presented to the top four or top six teams. MOW (Most Outstanding Wrestler) awards, if desired, may be presented to the top individual or the MOW in the lower weights and the MOW for the upper weight classes. Other possible tournament awards include Best Match (2 awards), Biggest Upset, and Best Official. A nice awards stand (with the tournament name and logo) adds class to the event. Make sure there is a set procedure for presenting awards. While some tournaments make the presentation a big event, others allow wrestlers to receive their medals at the scoring table immediately after their final match concludes. Traditionally, the champion receives a copy of the wall bracket as an added touch.

Concessions

A well-stocked concession stand (area) is important for two reasons. First, it is convenient for the fans and wrestlers. Spectators, parents, and wrestlers are not required to leave the premises to eat and don't have to deal with the problem of re-admittance. Inclement weather makes the concession stand even more valuable.

Secondly, concessions are tremendous fund raisers. A concession stand at an average size one day tournament can clear as much as $1000-$2000, but you must have what the people want, when they want it, at the appropriate temperature.

Wrestlers look for pastries, water, energy bars, energy drinks, and depending on the time between their matches, sub sandwiches. Parents look for 'meal' type foods (burgers, hot dogs, subs, pizza, sandwiches, chips, soups, cake, cookies, soft drinks, coffee, tea, water, hot chocolate). There is always a demand for candy and popcorn because of little brothers and sisters. Many tournament directors prefer table workers to receive a couple of coupons to be redeemed at the concession stand rather than have access to the hospitality room. Smaller one-day tournaments without a hospitality room provided concession stand coupons for officials, coaches, and table-workers. Adequate access to ice, heating devices (hot plates, microwave ovens, boilers), and refrigerators is mandatory. Make sure the area is left in the condition it was found (or even cleaner). Take an inventory of non-perishable items and store them for later use at dual meets or other tournaments.

Officials

Officials can 'make or break' the tournament. Frequently, associations assign referees to tournaments based on the level and quality of the competition. Secure the best group of officials available at a 3:2 ratio, three officials per two mats. This allows for rest breaks and hopefully better and more consistent officiating.

A committee member should be assigned to 'meet and greet' the officials and escort them to their dressing area immediately upon arrival. Provide a key so their valuables may be secured. If no key is available, assign a person to unlock and lock the door as needed. Towels and soap should be available in the shower area.

Officials should be informed of the 'weigh-in' area and have ample time to verify the certification of the scales to be used. Completed team weigh-in sheets must be presented to the official at weigh-ins each day of competition. Officials recommend one scale per three weight classes for large tournaments (16 man bracket).

Extra chairs need to be placed near the scorer's table for the 'resting' officials.

At the conclusion of the tournament, the appropriate forms for payment must be completed and forwarded to the athletic director.

Remember, if there is no hospitality room available you must provide food coupons for the officials to use at the concession stand between sessions.

First Aid/Athletic Training

The responsibility for administering first aid for injuries is primarily the responsibility of the school's athletic trainer and his student trainers. They should be advised of the date immediately after it is approved. A specified area should be designated to treat injuries with adequate room for training tables. Trainers are also responsible for setting up water containers for wrestlers to use.

If an adequate number of student trainers are available, one should be assigned to each mat to treat minor injuries, to stop bleeding, and to be responsible for blood cleanup. Trainers are considered tournament personnel and should have access to the hospitality room (or concession stand).

A cell phone should be available to call 911 in instances where very serious injury occurs.

Publicity

The Publicity Committee Chairman must have good interpersonal skills and ideally, a close relationship with the media in the community. A plan must be created for pre, during, and post tournament coverage. Newspapers, local TV stations, internet sites, and radio stations are usually the most available outlets for information. Pre-tourney releases should include the tournament name, date, time schedule, team entries, admission prices, key match ups, and any other facts that will create interest and increase attendance.

During the tournament, results should be provided to the available outlets. With today's technology, lap top computers enable us to provide immediate results to those unable to attend.

A post-tournament 'wrap-up' should include all individual and team results, plus special award winners.(MOW, Most Pins, Fastest Pin, etc). In addition to the aforementioned media, copies of the final results should be mailed to the coaches (hard copy or electronic) and provided to your school for announcement.

Finance

The Finance Committee is in charge of 'all things money'. This includes collecting, securing, recording, and depositing all the money involved. Included would be entry fees, gate (admissions), program sales, concession, and t-shirt sales. Expenditures must be logged including officials, awards, cleanup, supplies, security, concession supplies, program and t-shirt expenses. A Tournament Director fee may be required if the person is not a coach or volunteer.

A pre-tourney budget and a post-tourney spread sheet of all financial transactions should be developed and presented to the Takedown Club, tournament committee, and athletic director.

Security

In today's society, security is imperative for almost all athletic events. Due to the large crowds in attendance and the nature of competition, more than one security person is usually required. While some schools include athletic events in the duties of the SRO (School Resource Officers), others schools require event organizers to secure their own security personnel. One officer should be stationed near the entrance (gate) because of the money involved. A second officer should be stationed on 'the floor' to assure that only approved people are in the area. If available, a third officer should monitor the parking area to prevent break-ins and assist with parking.

In the event of controversy, officials should be escorted to their dressing area immediately at the tournament's conclusion.

Seeding (Optional)

If a seeding meeting is required for the tournament, the coach should work with the committee to discuss materials needed. Paper, entry lists, a copier, an overhead projector, pencils, numbers or cards, and brackets are most often the required items. Pizza, sandwiches, and drinks should be provided to the coaches by the Hospitality Committee.

Setup/Take down - The A-Team

It has been said that there are basically two types of horses in the world, show horses and workhorses. The A-Team (Allen) consists of the 'workhorses'. Lifting, loading, hauling, setup, cleaning, the actual running of the tournament, and the takedown and return of borrowed materials, is their responsibility.

Mats

After deciding on the number of mats required for competition, arrangements must be made to pick up mats to be borrowed. Make sure the mats are well-secured when transporting them between schools.

After unloading, set the mats up as required by the rule book. The green starting line MUST be on the official's right hand as he faces the scorer's table. Insure the mats provide the appropriate safety area to prevent injury.

Tape the mats securely and clean with approved cleansers. Clearly number the mats with 2" athletic tape covered with mat tape. The mat numbers should be approximately 18" to 24" in height for easy identification.

During the tournament, mats should be swept with a clean broom between sessions. The officials love it and even the wrestlers appreciate a clean mat. After the tournament, roll up the mats on the appropriate tubes and return to the appropriate school in accordance with prior arrangements.

Signs

A committee with the primary responsibility of making signs is helpful. The cheerleaders are often helpful in this area of work. Signs reading Entrance, Ticket Prices (adults, students, children under 6, tournament pass), Concessions, Weigh-In Area, Head Table, T-Shirts (price), Programs (price), Restrooms, Hospitality Room, Dressing Area, are usually necessary. Cheerleaders may also make a backdrop for the awards stand that includes the tournament name and logo.

Tables

A scoring table should be set up at a safe distance for each mat. Each table should have three chairs for the timer, a scorekeeper, and a 'flipper' (if flip charts are used). With current technology, some clocks keep match time, the score, and record injury time. Attempts should be made to secure the three-sided clocks as they reduce the number of table workers needed and are very visible to the spectators, participants, and coaches. For backup, stopwatches should be placed on each table. If actual match time is kept on a stop watch, another watch should be on each table to record injury/recovery time.

Also on the table should be materials for blood cleanup, paper towels, several sharpened pencils, red and green markers, and an extra set of ankle bands. Garbage cans need to be placed near each mat for disposal of hazardous materials and for wrestlers who need to spit or rinse their mouth.

Depending on the format used for mat assignment, a Match Tree and appropriate numbers may be required.

Table workers must secure the materials on the table between sessions. After the tournament, materials must be packed up and the table must be cleaned and folded. Tables should be returned to their storage area; other materials should be delivered to the head table.

Head Table

The 'head table' actually consists of three to four tables and ten to twelve chairs. The head table is the central hub of activity and information. Head table personnel are in charge of the opening ceremonies (National Anthem, Pledge of Allegiance), all announcements, printing match sheets and brackets, team scoring, updating wall brackets, presentation of awards, and the closing ceremony or comments.

The announcer is responsible for clearing the mats, reminding spectators of the sessions' starting times, reminding fans of the availability of concessions and t-shirts, announcing mat assignments (if necessary), and pointing out key matches in progress. He may also be required to announce award winners. The announcer may also play carefully screened upbeat music (Jock Jams) during warm up periods or between sessions.

Necessities for the head table include paper, a copier, a microphone for the PA system, a CD player with CD's, a copy of the brackets, match sheets, awards, wall brackets, a schedule of events, a list of key matches to watch, extra markers, extra pencils, extra extension cords, and staplers and staples.

It is vitally important to secure a good announcer. He should be energetic, enthusiastic, and knowledgeable of the sport and how tournaments are conducted. Announcements should include

The head table is responsible for making sure the tournament STARTS ON TIME.

After the tournament, all materials should be collected, packed, and returned to their appropriate storage area.

Evaluation

As soon as practical after the event, a meeting to evaluate the various areas of administration of the tournament should be held. Each committee must have the opportunity to provide input as to 'what went right' and 'what needs improvement'. The tournament director must them compile a list of the suggestions and make plans for improvement. Honest self-evaluation is a key to constant hosting a great tournament.

Thank You notes for those who donated, contributed, or supported are great public relations tools and also reap great benefits in the future.

What Coaches Like

Coaches like tournaments that:
Start on time.
Have good (or better) officiating.
Provide quality competition
Present nice awards.
Have an excellent hospitality room.
Make it easy to know where their wrestlers will wrestle.

What Parents Like

Parents like tournaments that:
Have affordable admission prices for the family.
Start on time.
Allow 'Little Johnny' (their son) to wrestle within the first couple of hours.
Have competent officials.
Enable them to see the match time and score.
Have a nice concession stand.
Provide nice awards (especially if 'Little Johnny' receives one).

What Wrestlers Like

Wrestlers like tournaments that:
Are properly seeded.
Provide competent officials.
Provide good competition.
Have stocked concession stands.
Make it easy to know their mat assignment.
Present great awards.

What Officials Like

Officials like tournaments that:
Provide a clean and secure dressing area.
Have quality wrestlers with discipline and sportsmanship.
Provide properly placed mats that are clean.
Competent coaches who display sportsmanship.
Provide proper paperwork for payment.
Have a great hospitality room.

Dual Meets, Tri-Meets, and Quadrangle Meets

As with tournaments, hosting any wrestling competition takes careful planning and organization. Meets are just tournaments on a smaller scale with the exception of awards, brackets, t-shirts, seeding, and a hospitality room. With experience, administration of competitions becomes routine and not as stressful as previously.

Tri-Meets can be run on one or two mats. On two mats, each team has wrestlers competing each round using the formats:

Tri-Meet Using One Mat

Round 1 A vs. B
Round 2 A vs. C
Round 3 B vs. C

Tri-Meet Using Two Mats

Round 1

Mat I Team A Lower Weights vs. Team B Lower Weights
Mat 2 Team A Upper Weights vs. Team C Upper Weights

Round 2

Mat 1 Team A Lower Weights vs. Team C Lower Weights
Mat 2 Team C Upper Weights vs. Team B Upper Weights

Round 3

Mat I Team A Upper Weights vs. Team B Upper Weights
Mat 2 Team C Lower Weights vs. Team B Lower Weights

The primary advantage of the preceding format is that all three teams get involved in the action immediately. The disadvantage is the format reduces the opportunity to build total team momentum.

Regular Team Quadrangle Meet (2 Mats Required)

Round I

Mat 1 A vs. B
Mat 2 C vs. D

Round 2

Mat 1 A vs. C
Mat 2 B vs. D

Round 3

Mat 1 A vs. D
Mat 2 B vs. C

Round Robin (Pool) Tournament

In a round robin tournament wrestlers are group into pools (usually 4, but can be 5 or 6). They wrestle everyone in their pool.

Allow coaches to FAX or email their entries with the athlete's exact weight after they weigh them in on Friday evening. This eliminates the need for a long tedious weigh-in process on Saturday morning, plus everyone is automatically 'on weight'.

This has proven to be a successful format with early season competition in the middle schools. Advantages of pool competition include:
Everyone gets a minimum of three matches in a short period of time.
Each wrestler (in a four man pool) receives a medal. Note: This is a great means of motivation for the beginning wrestler who is not fully committed yet.
Parents like to see their son wrestle several times in a single day.
Coaches usually love the format, as all their wrestlers are successful to some extent.
Round-robin competition eliminates the need for seeding.
Everybody 'makes weight'. (With grouping, no weight classes are needed.)

Regardless of the format used to administer competition, thorough planning, delegation of responsibility, and STARTING ON TIME are the keys to success.

CHAPTER 20

Promoting Your Wrestling Program via the Media

Declining attendance at wrestling events is a growing concern for coaches and athletic directors across the nation. Many coaches attribute this decline to the paucity of the rules that encourage action and increase excitement.

Could be, but I doubt it. I prefer to believe that the fault lies in the lack of promotion. In short, the key to enhancing fan interest does not lie in changing the rules, but in promoting the sport through the media. We must avail ourselves of every resource in promoting our program on the local, state, and yes, even the national level.

Some of the media have more significance than others in certain localities. Some are also more readily accessible than others. Regardless, we must strive to use those available in our particular situation.

State/National Television

Though coaches can rarely obtain team recognition on state or national television, they shouldn't hesitate to write or call the networks whenever they have a human-interest story or record worthy of the broad coverage. Television is a powerful means of promotion because of it's universal appeal.

Some stations are reserved specifically for educational purposes like GPTV (Georgia Public Television) and this possibility should be explored.

Cable TV

Preseason rules clinics and 'How to Watch' shows can be very beneficial in creating community interest. Common sense tells us that people are more likely to attend a sporting event if they understand the rules. Cable TV stations often enjoy broadcasting dual meets, tournament finals and highlights, and a post-season summary or tribute to the team.

The stations make money through sponsors' advertising, but the team members and coaches must be prepared to assume the workload involved in assembling materials that are essential for a successful program.

Radio

Radio provides one of the more immediately accessible means of reaching huge numbers of prospective fans at once. It is important for the coach to provide the announcer or sports announcer with a copy of the current team schedule so he may promote meets and tournaments in advance. With our busy society, people like to plan events days in advance.

'Call-In' talk shows or Saturday morning 'Week in Review' programs are extremely beneficial in creating interest. If the station is not able to cover an entire tournament match-by-match, delivering periodic live reports for the home fans is super.

The station may also be interested in sponsoring a 'Wrestler of the Week' spotlight detailing an individual's accomplishments and giving the community a few human interest facts about your team members.

A final suggestion regarding radio would be to get them to recognize an "All-Area' Wrestling Team composed of the best in your league, district, region, or area. The station would present plaques to the winners in recognition of their achievement. The kids will love the awards and the station will love the publicity creating a Win-Win situation.

Newspapers

Newspapers are also one of the more accessible and common forms of media for disseminating information. Newspapers reach a large audience and the publicity lasts longer than a TV program. A carefully planned series of releases and stories should be an important part of the preseason media plan.

'Picture Day' should include representatives from the newspaper's sports department and set at a time convenient for as many groups as feasible. If the school's photographer takes photos for the paper during competition during meets, he should keep two words in mind, ACTION and PEOPLE. Action photos are more appealing to viewers than 'stills' and it is better to focus on a few people rather than attempting to focus on many. Finally, such considerations as background, clarity, and significance should not be forgotten. Be sure to have names, weights, event, and the date on the back of all submitted photos.

Special stories and ideas should be mentioned or actually sent to the sport's director. Human interest stories are usually good ideas and enjoyable to read. If you have several brothers in your program, your team has a win streak, or your team is state or nationally ranked, make the most of it. Also, make the editor aware of any key meets or individual matches of community interest.

Keep the newspaper clippings on display in your school on a wall or bulletin board visible to the public. Posting the clippings is a great public relation tool.

Results of all competition should be 'called in' or FAXed by the team manager or scorekeeper, immediately after the event concludes. Newspapers want 'news', not old information from days ago. Pre-state tournament inserts are awesome promotional tools of promotion. The insert, usually a two-color job, should include photos, season records, individual season and career records, a team season summary, state schedule, directions to the tournament and other pertinent information available at press time. School newspapers provide 'in house' publicity and recognition as well, although the publications are not as frequently or current as regular newspapers.

Magazines / Periodicals

Of the thousands of magazines on the racks, few contain any articles on amateur wrestling.

Wrestling magazines are a must in your school's library. Most librarians are willing to subscribe to wrestling magazines and periodicals if requested to do so by a coach or group of team members. If the librarian is unable to subscribe for you, team rates are available when ordered in bulk.

My experience has been that wrestling magazines welcome and consistently ask for action photos, outstanding records, human-interest stories, and state tournament results. These are opportunities to promote your program that should not be neglected. Coaches should make an extra effort to nominate qualified individuals for All-American honors. Teams worthy of recognition in the Scholastic Dynasty section should be submitted without hesitation.

As a coach, you may bring recognition to your program by submitting technique articles to professional periodicals. The kids will get a great thrill from seeing their photos in a magazine, plus your school name and program will receive national publicity.

Videotapes/ DVDs

Plato is credited with saying, "A picture is worth a thousand words." I'm going on record as saying, "A videotape or DVD is worth 10,000 words". Both stimulate interest, command attention, and are an excellent means of disseminating information. Coaches may play the tapes or disks of the previous night's matches in the school lobby before school or in the cafeteria during lunch. The disks or tapes may also be reproduced and forwarded to the TV stations, as previously discussed, so excerpts may be broadcast.

Annual Program / Brochure

Football programs are a 'given' for teams at all levels. Wrestling programs are growing in popularity and not only do they promote your program, they can be an excellent fund raiser.

Programs (publications) may vary in size, quality, content, and organization, but should always be well-written, informative, and attractive.

After printing is completed, programs should be distributed to any or all of the following:

Board of Education members and your Superintendent, your school administration, faculty and staff, media outlets, middle school / junior high faculties and staff in your school district, sponsors, team members, visiting coaches and fans, college coaches, and support group members (booster clubs). Some coaches choose to sell the programs as a fund raiser, but I used it strictly for promotional purposes. They make excellent handouts when speaking at civic club meetings and at the yearly awards banquet for guests. Programs should be forwarded to national wrestling magazines for possible recognition. If your publication is recognized as one of the best, contact your local media for additional publicity. Secure several copies of the newspaper and send it, along with a brief 'Thank You' note to all purchasers of ads, the printer, and those responsible for creating it.

Posters

Posters, whether homemade or professionally printed will help promote your team. Posters should be colorful, attractive, simple, and send a message. The expression, "Sometimes less is more' applies to posters. Cluttered posters are often ignored, while simple posters can send a message even if the reader is just walking by and glances at them.

Posters can announce the opening date for practice, registration procedures, upcoming meets or tournaments, and even promote fund raisers. Poster contests are an excellent method of increasing awareness and creating excitement. Winners can be awarded Free Passes to home meets or tournaments as prizes. Remember to remove all posters immediately after the event has passed.

Lighted Signs

Messages on outdoor signs, lighted or unlit, flashing or non-flashing are viewed by thousands of motorists each day and are well worth the rental price. Sometimes the sign is the only reminder the fan will receive regarding the event. The messages must be short, simple, and to the point.

Gymnasium Name Boards

Basketball coaches have used the name boards for years to list their players and their numbers. The boards are inexpensive, easy to make (ask your shop for assistance), and provide needed publicity to all those who enter the gym. The booster club will readily purchase the material to make a couple for varsity and JV wrestling teams. Obviously, weight classes would replace the jersey number.

Award Sticker Programs

Several companies offer 'award sticker program' packages for individual recognition of wrestling achievement. Stickers are awarded for takedowns, pins, reversals, escapes, wins, etc. Placed in prominent places, these are excellent tools for creating interest and discussion about the team and individuals.

Schedules

An item as small as a pocket schedule, is a promotional device. It enables fans to stay informed of the competition dates with a quick glance. Larger poster placards with the opponent, date, and time should be posted throughout your school and community. A local business is always willing to print them if their logo is included.

T-Shirts

During the last few decades, T-shirts have become increasing popular as daily dress. In reality, T-shirts are 'walking billboards' used to present philosophies, themes, goals, accomplishments, and promote events. In addition to be excellent promotional items, they are great fund raisers.

School PA System and Closed Circuit TV

Technology has grown enormously in recent years. Nowadays, almost every high school broadcasts a daily closed-circuit TV program comprised of announcements, club meetings, weather, and sports.

Make sure the TV crew has all your results and has been provided footage of matches to be shown. Exciting moves can create interest and discussion and just might be a catalyst that gets a potential State Champion out for the team.

If a closed-circuit TV system is not available, use the 'old reliable', PA system to inform the student body of results. It is imperative that all announcements be creative, interesting, informative, and positive in nature.

Team Stationery

You probably never thought about items as small as a piece of stationery or 'Thank You 'card with a logo, as being promotional items, but they are. Each time you put the logo in front of a person, you are promoting your program. Use the letterhead for all correspondence related to your team. Finally, never forget that a small 'Thank You' is always appreciated and can reap great benefits.

Self-Evaluation

At the season's conclusion, sit down with your assistants, booster club representatives, and athletic director to engage in a detailed self-evaluation regarding promotion. Some strategies and techniques may require only minor changes, some may need to be drastically changed or even eliminated, while others may remain as they were. If continuous progress is expected, self-evaluation should be regular and through.

CHAPTER 21

Producing an Award-Winning Publication

Wrestling publications are excellent public relations tools and can be effective fund raisers. With teamwork and planning, an award-winning publication can become a reality.

The first step in producing the publication is to decide the purpose. Is it strictly for public relations? Is it primarily a fund raiser? Is it a combination of both?

If the main purpose is to raise revenue, the program will have many ad pages and few pages of information. Conversely, if public relations and program promotion are your primary objectives, information pages will be greater than ad pages. Properly planned programs can meet both objectives as desired.

First, the editor and committee chairpersons must meet with the printer to decide on the cost per program, number of pages, number of pages with color, cover and centerfold alternatives, due date for delivering information, expected publication date, accepted method of payment, and the medium to be used for presenting ads, photos and information.

As with tournaments, work by committees is the best way to achieve your goal. Recommended committees are: cover design and theme, ad sales, photograph, articles and information, distribution.

Cover Design Committee

The cover design should be attractive and attention-getting whether black and white or full color. The design can be as simple as the team name (school), the team mascot, the year, and the cost. Even if the programs are distributed free of charge, a price should be on the cover. Many schools like the cover to reflect the team's theme for the season.

The centerfold is usually the focal point as the program naturally opens there. The team photo or a duplicate of the team's theme poster usually makes an attractive centerfold.

Ad Sales Committee

This committee should consist of people who enjoy sales and have excellent public relations skills, but are also able to take 'no' for an answer. Establish a sales goal and get the entire club involved. 'Everybody knows somebody' and they should call on these people for support. Potential ad purchasers to be contacted by parents are: their insurance agents, the guy who just sold them a new car, the owners of restaurants they frequent, business associates, the real estate agent who sold them their house, their barber or beautician, their spa or gym owner, the local grocery store manager, their primary clothing store, their bank, their tire store owner.

Parents often like to purchase a page, or portions of a page, to honor their son. These ads may contain his baby photo, action shots taken throughout his career, a message from the parents, or 'that cute photograph' they wish to share.

The entire community and booster club are filled with potential buyers. Don't hesitate to call on them to support their local athletes.

Photograph Committee

With the recent popularity of the digital camera and it's simplicity in use, professional photographers are no longer a requirement for quality pictures. Parents that are avid photographers are usually willing and eager to participate on this committee.

Possible posed photos include; head shots of all wrestlers, managers, score keepers, trainers, all wrestling coaches, and the athletic director. Group photos of the school administrations, the Board of Education, the varsity, JV, middle school and youth teams, parents, and the booster club officers are also a basic requirement.

Action shots from the previous season may be obtained from local sports editors, school yearbook photographers, and most parents. Communicate carefully with the printer, as some require the photos to be submitted on discs for better quality and the ease of transfer.

Articles and Information Committee

The list of possible articles, letters, cartoons, and technical information is practically endless.

After the planning stage of the program is concluded however, a definite number of pages for articles and information should have been determined. It is the responsibility of the committee to carefully select the information to be printed, organize it in a logical fashion, and prepare it to be submitted as required by the printer.

Though there is no required order of material, the following Table of Contents is a suggested arrangement for consideration.

Letter from the Superintendent (Board of Education photo)
Letter from the Principal (Photo of School Administration)
Letter from the Booster Club President (Photo of Booster Club Officers)
Head Coach Biography (Photo)
Assistant Coaches Biographies (Photos)
Message to our Seniors (Group Photo of Seniors)
Senior Photos and Sketches
Junior Photos and Sketches
Sophomore Photos and Sketches
Freshmen Photos and Sketches
Photos of Scorekeepers, Managers, Trainers, Support Personnel
Baby Photos
Shout Out Ads (patrons)
Action Shots
Letter to Parents, Random Photos of Parents
Previous Year's Results
Wrestling Schedules
"How to Watch a Match" Article
Rule Changes (optional)
Weight Loss Humor
Wall of Fame (previous stars)
Advertisements

When designing the layout of the program, remember the number of pages must be divisible by four, including the front and back covers.

Distribution Committee

After publication, programs must be distributed with an organized strategy. Complimentary programs may be given to any or all of the following; ad purchasers, parents, wrestlers and team personnel (all levels), Board of Education, schools administrators, athletic directors.

Several programs must be reserved to enter in national wrestling publication contests.

If the primary purpose of the program is public relations and team recognition, distribute several programs to places where people sit, wait and read. Medical offices, dentist offices, bus stations, and teacher lounges are excellent examples of places meeting this criteria.

Get organized, plan, be creative, have fun, follow through to the finished product. The benefits of producing an award winning publication and its impact on the total wrestling program are immeasurable, but well worth the effort.

CHAPTER 22

Ten Ways to Increase Attendance At Home Meets

Developing community support and increasing home crowd attendance takes a lot of planning, and a little creativity. Through the years, I have assembled several techniques that insure a larger crowd at meets. All aren't moneymakers initially, but are not costly either. The key to a growing fan base is getting them there the FIRST time - then most will be hooked for life. From my observations, few people go to sporting events alone. They want a friend to go as well so when you get one you usually get two or more. The number multiplies even more when the event involves younger kids.

1. FREE Pre-Season Rules Clinic and Intra-squad Meet.

   Conduct a pre-season intra-squad dual meet before the first official competition of the season. Some coaches may prefer to make it the final wrestle-off for the varsity and JV starting slots. This event will usually draw crowds of fans who are eagerly anticipating the season opener and parents of the competitors attending for support.

   Prior to the meet, the coach may choose to hold a pre-season "Rule's Clinic'" where the general public is invited to learn about the sport of wrestling. Demonstrating basic moves from each position after explaining the scoring system will reap great rewards. An educated fan is a happy and more enthusiastic fan. If the official is willing to explain his role (safety, awarding points, signals) allow him to do so. This is an excellent opportunity to address sportsmanship on the part of fans and wrestlers. A brief question and answer session can be helpful. A brochure explaining the rules, picturing the referee's signals, and including the season schedule should be distributed.

2. Elementary / Middle School / Junior High Wrestler Recognition Night

   Holding an elementary, middle, or junior high team recognition night will often be the greatest single event for increasing attendance. First, there are usually a large number of kids to be invited and they DO NOT DRIVE! One or both parents will usually stay for the meet, and sometimes all the brothers and sisters. If the visiting team is willing, a couple of exhibition matches at each level may be wrestled. The wrestlers and their parents could be seated together in a specific section of the gym or on the mat edge (legal distance, of course). An event of this type provides positive reinforcement and motivation to all youth wrestlers, regardless of their current skill level. They begin to dream about the day when they'll be high school 'State Champions'.

3. Teacher Appreciation Night

    For academic and athletic reasons, support of the faculty is imperative. It's a lot better for the coach to hear that 'Little Johnny' is not turning in his work or behaving properly from the teacher than from an administrator who has suspended him or a counselor who has posted his failing grade. Faculty-coach relations are some of the most important you'll ever develop. A social before the meet featuring snacks and drinks and special seating near the mat will reap great benefits. The teachers to be recognized will usually bring their spouse and often the entire family.

4. Kids Free Night

    A 'Kid's Free Night' (12 years and under) can pack the gym if properly promoted. It's similar to the youth wrestler recognition event, but it is open to all youth. This is a great way to expose every kid in the community to a great sport and perhaps recruit a few new competitors for the youth teams. Once again, the parents will usually stay, plus the concession stand sales will boom.

5. Wrestler's Choice—Pick Five

    Give each wrestler on the team (all levels) five free tickets. They are allowed to give them to friends, neighbors, or classmates of their choice. As in previous examples, they will probably bring another friend, but will help concession sales regardless.

6. Senior Recognition Night

    Senior Recognition Night should be a most memorable promotion. Find an opponent that you will probably beat with all your seniors in the lineup. Before the warm-ups begin, introduce each senior and, if permitted, present a Senior Appreciation plaque to each for outstanding contributions to the program. If you have more than one senior in a weight class, arrange exhibition matches if allowable under your state association guidelines for each. Also include managers, trainers, and scorekeepers in the recognition festivities.

7. Parents Appreciation Night

    To express appreciation to the parent's and/or guardians for their efforts in making your program successful, have a Parents Appreciation night. Before each match, introduce the parents of the competing wrestler. Present the mom with a rose and the dad with a handshake. Allow them to sit at mat side (with the official's permission) or as close to the mat as allowable. A pre-meet social would be a nice touch and an opportunity to recruit Takedown Club members.

8. Spirit Night

    For Spirit Night, invite the Spirit Band, cheerleaders, dance team and step team. Arrange performances (3-4 minutes in length) by the invited groups between JV and Varsity competition. Boyfriends, girlfriends, parents, and relatives will pack the house and as usual, concession sales will rise.

9. $5 Family Night Special

    The entire family attends for $5.00. More people will attend, it's very affordable, and the concession stand will be raking in the money all night long. Hold a drawing to give away a donated family vacation during the event.

10. Alumni Homecoming Night

    Host an Alumni Homecoming Night during a home dual meet in which wrestling alumni are the special guests. Recognize all wrestling alumni in attendance, and give special recognition to state champions, state place-winners, and former coaches. Try to schedule a previous rival which will be more meaningful to alumni, and also create community interest.

CHAPTER 23

Fund Raising: A Necessary Evil

Unfortunately, in many communities, fund raisers are absolute necessities to supplement budget shortfalls or to finance special trips and events for wrestling teams. The increasing costs of officials, uniforms, travel, security, and equipment make raising money a 'necessary evil' for all but the wealthiest of programs. Many coaches love to travel 'out of state' to promote their programs and athletes or seek out tough competition and need additional funds. Following the suggestions, guidelines, and tips' listed, you can put the 'FUN' and 'FUND' back into fund raising with few problems.

A few tips for successful fund raising events:

1. Limit the number of fund raisers per season. Some school districts limit them for you, but it may be necessary, as coach, to be the self-regulating agent for your boosters. Schedule the events so as not to conflict with another fund raiser at your school if at all possible, especially if they involve sales.

2. Set definite and limiting time-frames as well as solid financial goals. When fundraising events drag on for weeks, the enthusiasm dwindles, burnout is more likely to occur, and record keeping becomes more difficult. Keep your people 'fired-up' and energetic, keep good records, and as Larry the Cable guy said so eloquently, 'Git-R-Done'.

3. Plan, Plan, Plan and Promote, Promote, Promote! Let the entire school and community know the what, when, where, and why of the event. If people know that it is for a special out-of-state tournament, badly need equipment, or new uniforms, they are more likely to be supportive.

    Send emails or letters home to parents, make posters and display them in high-traffic areas, and get as much media coverage as possible.

4. Monitor those who are allowed to handle the money. Keep accurate records of the amount of products issued, sold, paid for, and returned. While we all would like to think that our peers are honest and reliable, unfortunately, many are not. Many booster clubs have been torn apart and landed in court because of poor record keeping and a lack of accountability. The Project Chairman or Treasurer should present a financial statement to the club members immediately after the event concludes and all funds collected.

5. Vary workers when possible. Some clubs are blessed to have enthusiastic, energetic, and seemingly tireless workers. Be very careful, however, not to allow them to end up with the dreaded FRBOB (Fund Raiser Burn-Out Blues). Get as many volunteers signed up for your planned projects as possible and let them 'share the load'. A kind word of appreciation, a simple card, or special recognition at the next booster club meeting will reap great rewards.

Six Safety Suggestions for Young Fund Raisers

Younger athletes are often required to be active participants in raising money in the community. Due to our present societal conditions, a special focus on child safety is imperative.

The following suggestions are guidelines to protect our most valuable resource:

1. NEVER allow young athletes to sell door to door to strangers alone. Parents should ALWAYS accompany them in these situations.

2. Remind them of STRANGER DANGER and instruct them to never talk to strangers alone—EVER!

3. NEVER allow young athletes to carry large amounts of money.

4. Limit sales by youth to the daylight hours. There's danger after dark from vehicles and people.

5. Allow younger athletes to sell over the phone and by email whenever possible.

$$$ Ideas That Can Rake in the Cash $$$

Most fund raisers involve selling, providing services, direct donations, or entertainment. The number of fund raisers is almost unlimited and I would never suggest my list is complete. My Takedown Club has used several of the following ones over the years, with varying degrees of success.

Discuss the ideas with your boosters and decide which are most appropriate for your community.

Sales: Product sales are one of the more frequently used methods used to raise money. Regardless of the items sold, record keeping, accountability, promotion, and a respectable profit margin are of critical importance. Items that may, and have been sold for a profit are:

Seeds (flowers, vegetables)
Pizzas (coupons, 2 for 1)
Discount Cards (restaurants, movies, car washes)
Spirit Items (shirts, caps, shorts, visors, sweatshirts)

Candy (M & M's, bars, lollipops)
Popcorn
Fruit
Air Fresheners (auto, home)
Cookies
Cookie Mixes
Scented Candles
Christmas Trees
Christmas Tree Ornaments
Christmas Wreaths
Christmas Cards
Poinsettias
Wrapping Paper (assorted)
Coffees
Teas
Jerky (beef, buffalo)
Stationery
Nuts
Magazines (subscription sales)
Pretzels
Program Ads
Windup Flashlights
Auto Safety Kits
Home First Aid Kits
Home Fire Extinguishers

Cakes

Services: Service-oriented fund raisers have several advantages. Primarily, the item being sold is a service as opposed to a tangible product so basically there is nothing to keep up with, except the cash.

Car Washes
Rent a Kid
Windshield Wash (Squeegee)
Dog Walking
Dog Washes
Raking Leaves
Grocery Bagger for A Day (Bagging For Buck$)
Spray House Numbers on Curbs
Gas Station Attendant

Entertainment: Entertainment fund raisers are very popular and primarily have a tremendously high margin of profit. (A few events may require minimum expenses for awards, supplies, and officials.)

Student-Faculty Competitions (softball, basketball, volleyball)
Dances (homecoming, winter holiday, spring)
Talent Shows
Tournaments (preseason takedown, chess)
Car Shows
Cheerleader Competitions
Horse Shows
Fall Clinics / Summer Camps
Halloween Haunted House
Halloween Costume Party / Dance
Fall Festivals
Donkey Basketball Game
Chili Cook Off
Bingo Night
Poker Tournament
Turkey Shoot

Others:

A-Thons: (takedown, walk, jog, lift, jump, rock, bike, tricycle)
Flamingo Fun
Snowman Poop
Recycling Drives (aluminum cans, print cartridges)
Raffles
Yard / Garage Sales
Ebay Consignment Sales
Alumni membership Drives

Daniel's Fund Raising Favorites

Most Creative: Snowman Poop Sales

During the pre-Christmas holidays, go in front of a Wal-Mart or other local store (with permission) and sell small Zip-Loc bags of 4-5 large marshmallows for $2.00 with a colorful note attached that says, "You've been really naughty, so here's the scoop; All you get for Christmas is this snowman poop". Many people will enjoy buying this inexpensive gag gift for that 'special' relative, family member, boss, friend, classmate, or co-worker and the bucks add up quickly.

What a way to spread holiday cheer!

Most Money for the Least Work: Weight Class Sponsors

My Takedown Club used this idea to raise $7000 in less than a month. Here's how it works. Takedown Club members go out into the community and solicit businesses, clubs, fans, or groups of relatives to sponsor their son's weight class for the season at a cost of $250. (You choose amount that is appropriate for your needs and the available resources). Almost everyone had little trouble in finding at least one sponsor. Some energetic boosters are able to solicit more than one sponsor.

These sales are used to cover the weight classes for those people who don't get the job done. Key targets for sponsorships are: Insurance companies where parents have been buying insurance for years, car dealers where the person last purchased a car, the realtor who sold them their home, supermarkets where the person has shopped for years, military branches who have almost unlimited federal funds for advertising, former wrestlers who want to sponsor their own weight class, banks where the person has an account, favorite restaurant that you have patronized for years, business partners, alumni, groups of friends, and your own company. We even had a group of relative chip in a few bucks each and call the sponsorship, "Dusty's Fan Club". Don't hesitate to ask for support from those whom you have supported for years.

In return for their support, the sponsors get:

1. Their name or business listed on the back of the team T-shirt as an Official Sponsor.

2. Their name and/or logo on the team website.

3. Their name or business announced at all home meets and tournaments.

4. Free T-shirts (We allow them to get 4-5 for employees)

5. A sign posted in the gymnasium with the business logo or name.

6. Free admission to all home events.

Most Fun: Flamingo Flocking Fun

Purchase 10 pink plastic flamingos (lawn decorations). Pick 10 yards in your community to be the lucky (or unlucky) recipients. Attach a card to the flamingos' neck with a phone number and all the pertinent information regarding your groups' project. Explain that for a $10 donation, the flamingo will be removed from their yard, but for $15 it will be moved to the neighbor's lawn of their choice, and for $20 they'll be insured against its return for the entire year. (Always allow for the option of free pick up with no donation for those without a good sense of humor.) This is a fairly new project, but can be lots of fun for everyone. It takes a little organization, but is well worth the effort. An additional fund raising idea is to sell "Pink Power Insurance" in advance to boosters to prevent the pink visitor from landing in their yard.

Newest: Ebay—Internet Sales

Due to the sale of millions of dollars worth of goods on the internet, the idea has spread to the school fund raising arena. Boosters, parents, or businesses donate items to be listed on the internet for sale.

Advantages of the internet sales over yard sales include:

1. Internet sales are not affected by the weather.

2. Your market immediately becomes the world.

3. Donations may continue all season long.

4. Items are 'For Sale' longer than a few hours on a Saturday.

5. Due to the bidding process, you receive 'top dollar' for the items listed.

Donations, listings, and sales may be only for a limited period of time (month, or so) or the club may decide to make it an on-going project. The listing fees may be donated by the person listing the items or the club should reimburse him for actual expenses. Buyers always pay for shipping and handling. The price of packaging materials should be included in the S/H fees.

CHAPTER 24

Wrestling Officials and How to Deal With Them

Officials are a vital part of our sport and have specific responsibilities and obligations. They are responsible for maintaining standards of competition and enforcing the rules and regulations that govern the sport. In general, they must:

* ensure safe competition in a safe environment

* start and stop action when required

* award points to competitors

* assess and enforce penalties on wrestlers and coaches when necessary

* establish and maintain rapport with coaches and athletes

It's been said that the nature of relationships between wrestling coaches and wrestling officials is due to one big difference in their points of view: coaches care who wins and officials don't care. The relationship between the two groups is often complicated and is often described as resembling that between siblings: love-hate, cooperative-competitive, protective-rejecting, respect-disdain.

Perhaps that is true in the wrestling family, but like many families, the things that coaches and officials have in common outweigh any perceived differences. Both groups love their sport and both groups want the wrestlers to compete in a safe environment. Regardless of the conflict, however, it can usually be resolved if both sides approach it in the right manner.

Suggestions for Success with Officials

* As a coach, realize you will not agree with every call by the official, but also realize that your reaction to poor calls is something you can control. At the appropriate time, ask questions in a reasonable tone that relate to rule application and not questions of judgment.

* Know the rules and be extra familiar with any recent rule changes or new interpretations.

* Make use of any formal mechanisms in your sport for raising officiating issues.

* Understand that once a call is made, questioned, and a final decision has been made, it does no good to continue the discussion. Focus on the situation at hand and leave the last call alone.

* Be realistic about expectations of officials during sporting events, especially rookies. Rarely is a match ever wrestled, coached or officiated perfectly.

* Encourage wrestlers to shake hands with the officials and thank them after a competition has concluded.

10 Things to Avoid Saying to Officials

"This Must Be Your First Tournament".

"Officiating Will Be Easier If You'll Learn The Rules".

"Where Are All The Competent Officials Today?"

"If You'll Stop Him From Backing Up, We'll Take Him Down".

"I Need To Get My Sun Glasses; His Backup Lights Are Blinding Me"

"They're Making Rule Books In Braille Next Season".

"If You Had Been In Position, You Would Have Seen The Nearfall".

"We Need A Timeout To Put Our Track Shoes On If You're Going To Make Us Chase Him".

"We Are On Bloopers And Practical Jokes, Right"?

"You Wouldn't Recognize Stalling If It Hit You In The Head".

I've been guilty of making all these comments during my thirty-five year coaching career. Some officials accepted them as humorous and 'all in fun', others reacted slightly differently and I was immediately asked to leave the gym.

The old saying, "We can't live with them and we can't live without them" has never been more applicable than when discussing wrestling officials. They are here to stay and the smart coaches will learn to 'live with them' harmoniously.

CHAPTER 25

Absolute Truths for Wrestlers

A Baker's Dozen

As a high school, college, and Freestyle-Greco-Roman wrestler, I discovered several 'Absolute Truths' in the universe that apply specifically to wrestlers. It is important to have a clear understanding of each to avoid making the same mistakes that I made during my career.

1. Winning Is More Fun Than Losing

   Research has shown that athletes at all levels enjoy the 'Thrill of Victory' much more than suffering with 'The Agony of Defeat'. The point to be made here is that in the end paying the price to attain victory is worth the effort.

2. It's Okay to Be Tired

   Fatigue is necessary to get in condition for optimal performance. Rather than whining about how tired you are, be thankful that you have been blessed with good health and the ability to participate in athletics. There are kids all across America that would give anything to have the opportunity you have. 'Tired' is a small step toward the superior conditioning that is a vital asset in competition.

3. Most Headaches are all In Your Head

   Don't be surprised if you develop a headache during practice. People are 'pounding' on your head, your heart is pumping fast, you're straining, you're stressing . . . . a slight headache is to be expected. If you suffer from serious headaches such as migraines or get a mild or serious concussion in practice, take the proper precautions and tell your coach or a trainer, otherwise, live with it.

4. There Is a Difference between 'Hurting' and 'Being Hurt'

   Rarely, but sometimes, wrestlers suffer serious injuries that require medical attention. Missing practice with a doctor's (trainer) note due to actually 'being hurt' is understandable and non-negotiable. It is important to realize, however, that all injuries do not require a complete lack of activity. Those with shoulder, elbow, wrist, or hand injuries may be able to jog, or

269

ride a stationary bike, for example. If you are hurting because of bumps, bruise, mild strains, busted lips, black eyes, or a bloody nose, just remember that you are only 'hurting' and not really 'hurt' (injured).

5. It's Okay to Bleed

Unfortunately, bleeding is an unavoidable part of all contact sports. However, it's okay to bleed within reason. Bloody noses, busted lips, cuts and scratches are to be expected. For the non-serious occasions like those requiring immediate medical attention, stop practicing, have the trainer stop the bleeding, clean up (change blood-stained shirts, clean the mat), cover the wound or plug the nose (if necessary) and return to battle immediately.

6. There Is a Tendency to Focus on the Negative

After consulting with psychics, soothsayers, and psychiatrists, I have discovered that this tendency in athletics is completely unexplainable. Although 99.9% of their body feels great, wrestlers tend to focus on a little discomfort (bruise, cut, black eye, blister, jammed finger, muscle strain, mat burn, stomachache,) that only takes up the remaining .1% of it. Under these circumstances, the key to a successful practice or match is to re-direct your attention and focus on the end results and the positive aspects of working hard.

7. Wrestling Practice Ain't Disneyland

I'm sure we've all had kids come to us ready to quit with the excuse, "It's just not fun anymore".

Well, here's a news flash for all the wrestlers with this attitude, "You want fun? Go to Disneyland." Although we all enjoy a variety in drills and games with a little humor sprinkled in, practice cannot consist entirely of fun and games. If wrestling was all 'fun and games', the practice room would be so crowded that practice would be nearly impossible. Becoming a champion requires dedication, hard work, repetitive drill (often boring), and sacrifices. The 'fun' part comes when you step on the top level of the awards stand.

8. Some Individuals Are Not As Tough As Their Reputation

Every coach has dealt with a wrestler who was 'psyched out' immediately after seeing his opponent. "Aw, man, I have to wrestle Dusty Daniel" or "I'll lose my first match for sure" or "I can't beat him", they'll say. Even though the opponent may be a State Champion or be undefeated, he is still human. He can be beaten on a given day. I always point out the match where Olympic Gold Medalist and wrestling great, Dan Gable, lost his last match in college when no one thought it was possible. "You don't wrestle the reputation, you wrestle the person", I say.

9. Six Minutes on Your Feet Are Longer Than Six Minutes On The Mat

Though this fact goes against all theories of keeping time, it is true. This 'truth' cannot be proven by a stopwatch, but can be easily be verified by actual competition. On your feet, there's no chance to rest or 'catch your breath' like there is down on the mat where hand control and lying flat provides this opportunity. Only a superior conditioned wrestler can attack his opponent in the neutral position for the entire match.

10. The Hardest Part of Practice Is Getting Dressed

It has been said that "The longest journey begins with the first step". The same is true for wrestling practice. Guys often sit around the locker room dreading practice and hesitating to get dressed in workout gear. Consequently, they are late or end up telling the coach they don't feel well or don't think they can practice that day. Supervising the locker room daily and encouraging the guys to 'hustle up' and get on the mat can help solve most problems. I ask those who say they really don't feel like practicing to 'get dressed and do what you can'. Many, after warming up, have gone on to have great practices.

11. 'Sick' People Are In the Hospital; 'Feeling Bad' People Should Be At Practice

Wrestlers have approached me the day after missing or 'skipping' practice and say "I was sick".

"What hospital did you go to?" I ask. Usually the response is, "None, I was at home"." Well, you weren't really sick then", I say, "You were only feeling bad". "Isn't this an over simplification", you might ask? Perhaps, but the point is there. Unless the wrestler is in the hospital, has a contagious disease, or doctor's orders to stay home, he should be at practice. With most minor injuries and skin-related problems, the athlete is still able to go through some type of workout like jogging or riding a stationary bike to maintain conditioning.

12. Internal Celebration of Victory Is Best

Since my family purchased our first television when I was nine years old (1957), I have watched in awe as professional athletes celebrated championships. Even as a child, I couldn't figure out what piling on top of each other, spraying champagne in everyone's face or pouring it on their heads, and holding up the '#1' finger had to do with winning. I remember asking my Dad, "Why do they have to hold up one finger? Everyone knows the champions are always #1."

It is my opinion that 99% of the outward celebration antics are strictly for 'show' and not sincere. My policy has always been to instruct teams to accept victory humbly, shake the opponents' hands, quietly accept the trophy and go home as CHAMPIONS. They should pose for photos with class. How the team celebrates on the bus and away from the crowd is a different story. After the meet or tournament, let the fans do all the cheering, clapping, and celebrating. As my assistant coach, Beasey Hendrix, reminded our team on several occasions, "Act like we did what we came to do and not like it was a surprise". Never allow wrestlers to hold up one finger or lay in the floor for photos. Fans, yours and others, will be very impressed by the 'class' you exhibit.

13. Not Everyone Loves a Winner

While we would love to think that everyone does love a winner, the fact is they don't—especially losers and those filled with jealousy. The important thing is that people respect you and recognize your accomplishments. Want people to like you? Send flowers and candy. Want people to respect you? Beat 'em on the mat!